DATE DUE

APR 19 1976			
GAYLORD			PRINTED IN U.S.A.

The Meaning of McCarthyism

Second Edition

Edited and with an introduction by

Earl Latham
Amherst College

D. C. HEATH AND COMPANY
Lexington, Massachusetts   Toronto   London

Published simultaneously in Canada.

Printed in the United States of America.

International Standard Book Number: 0-669-81851-8

Library of Congress Catalog Card Number: 72-14041

CONTENTS

Sociological Critiques

Political Critiques

V McCARTHYISM: TWO CONCLUSIONS

INTRODUCTION

The national turmoil over the Communist movement which occurred in America in the late forties and early fifties had its beginnings in two developments in the 1930s. The first was the expansion of the federal government to give effect to the new concepts of economic regulation and social service associated with the New Deal. The second was the change in the political line of the world Communist movement, a change from a policy of hostile attack against the institutions of liberal democratic government to one of seeming cooperation with all agencies of social reform. The symbol of this temporary friendship was the popular front and, for some, it doubtless gave the Communist movement credentials of respectability. Membership in the Communist party increased, and with the expansion of the federal civil service, some members of the party found employment in government agencies.

Although liberal toleration of the Communist movement in those years was often to provoke the charge that liberals were fellow-travelers of the CPUSA, the truth is that the Communist party was the fellow-traveler of American progressivism for a short while, just as it was to become the fellow-traveler of midwestern isolationism for a short while. Popular front amiability disappeared when the Nazi-Soviet Pact of 1939 cleared the way for the invasion of Poland and for almost two years the American Communist party opposed American defense preparations. With the German invasion of the Soviet Union in June 1941 and the Japanese attack upon the United States in December, the Communist line changed from antagonism to collaboration for the duration of the war, and then back to antagonism when the war was over.

Even at the height of the Communist activity in the popular front period, however, official steps were taken to control some aspects of the movement. In the Hatch Act of 1938, membership in the Communist party was made a ground for refusal of federal employment. In 1938 the House Committee on Un-American Activities was established. In 1940, the Smith Act made it a federal offense for anyone to advocate the violent overthrow of the government. Investigations by the executive agencies into the loyalty of persons in federal employment were begun as early as 1941. In 1947 the first general loyalty program was established by executive order throughout the federal establishment. Measures, in short, were developed for the unostentatious treatment of questions of loyalty and security through administrative action, although it was Congress, not the executive branch, that took the initiative.

From 1938 to 1948, however, the problem of Communists in federal employment increasingly became involved with two other concerns—the hostility of conservatives toward the New Deal and the independence of the Congress from the executive branch. Anti-New Dealers were not always scrupulously careful to distinguish between liberals and Communists, and some made great effort to embarrass the administration through attacks that seemed to say that subversion and social reform were the same thing. Conservative hostility concentrated in a coalition of Republicans and Southern Democrats in Congress. When they combined, their majority then made Congress competitive with the executive.

The heat in these partisan tensions, already high in 1946 and 1947, became feverish in 1948. In July of that year, Whittaker Chambers and Elizabeth Bentley testified about the existence of two independent espionage rings which had been working for the Soviet Union in Washington for years, and Chambers named Alger Hiss, a former high official of the State Department, as one of his partners in espionage. Chambers repeated his accusations outside the immunity of the congressional hearing. Hiss sued Chambers for libel, and Chambers produced documents that tended to support his accusation. Hiss was then prosecuted for perjury in denying certain connections with Chambers, and was eventually convicted.

The Hiss–Chambers scandal did not become a controversy between President Truman and Thomas Dewey in the campaign of 1948, although secondary figures in both parties made something of the Communist issue. Perhaps the debate in these respects was not pressed as hard as it might have been because of the almost universal expectation that the Republicans were going to win the election anyway. The news media, the poll-takers, and political leaders in both parties supposed that a new regime, at last, would end the New Deal hegemony of sixteen years. But the change did not occur. Although the electorate confusedly indicated that it was in favor óf a change of some sort (no candidate received a majority of the popular votes), there was no clarity about the nature of the change desired, and no clear delegation to either party to make it. The conservative coalition in Congress pursued courses independent of the president in domestic matters during the second term of President Truman and stepped up the investigation of the Communist movement in government circles and elsewhere in the nation.

It was at this point that Senator Joseph R. McCarthy became a focus of the uproar over Communists in federal employment. In February 1950, he charged that the Department of State knowingly harbored Communists, and for months the press was filled with the acrimony of the argument that ensued. In this verbal combat with the State Department and others, Senator McCarthy quickly established the style of contention that was to be admired (or condoned) by his supporters and to be deplored and even feared by his opponents, a style of which the principal elements were recklessness in accusation, careless inaccuracy of statement, and abuse of those who criticized him. Hearings on the McCarthy charges were held under the chairmanship of Senator Millard Tydings of Maryland, whose committee exonerated the State Department. Critics called the proceedings a "whitewash."

Other events of 1950 illustrate the force of the new fury over the Communist issue, midway between the elections of President Truman and President Eisenhower. The Supreme Court upheld the conviction of the eleven top leaders of the Communist party under the Smith Act of 1940. The Court also refused to review the convictions of two Hollywood writers who had declined to answer questions about possible Communist connections. Judith Coplon of the Department of Justice was convicted of conspiracy with a Soviet representative at the United Nations (later reversed on procedural grounds). Harry Gold, David Greenglass, and Julius and Ethel Rosenberg were arrested on various charges connected with atomic espionage. A grand jury brought indictments against individuals involved in the transfer of hundreds of secret and other classified documents from the State Department to the offices of a relatively obscure journal called *Amerasia.*

The storms of controversy blew just as hard for the next two years. Early in 1951, the McCarran subcommittee seized the files of the Institute of Pacific Relations and began a long investigation into the relations between the institute and the Department of State, relations which were thought by the committee to involve subversion. The Rosenberg trial opened in March, and in April the Rosenbergs were sentenced to death. The head of the FBI assured Congress that his organization was ready to arrest 14,000 dangerous Communists in the event of war with the Soviet Union. A foundation offered $100,000 to support research into the creation of a device for detecting traitors.

At the beginning of 1952, Senator William Benton of Connecticut tried to have the United States Senate expel Senator McCarthy. In April, Senator McCarthy offered a resolution for a full-scale investigation into Senator Benton's official, business, and personal activities. In the presidential campaign in the fall of 1952, the Communist issue was given greater prominence than it had had in 1948. Richard Nixon said that Adlai Stevenson had disqualified himself for the presidency by providing a character reference for Alger Hiss at the latter's trial for perjury. Twenty-two prominent lawyers, some of them Eisenhower supporters, upheld Stevenson. Sixteen other lawyers issued a public statement that contradicted the position taken by the twenty-two. General Eisenhower accused the Truman administration of having permitted spies of the Soviet Union to steal secrets. Senator McCarthy made a widely advertised television speech in which he used "Alger" for "Adlai" in faked mistake. Although the change of regime that was voted in 1952 was impelled by deeper forces than the rhetoric of the national campaign, "Communism" was certainly one of the symbols under which it occurred.

The first year of the Eisenhower era saw McCarthy at his peak. In the second he was brought down and condemned. In 1953, Senator McCarthy, now chairman of the Senate Government Operations Committee, conducted an investigation of the Voice of America and the overseas information programs of the State Department, with destructive roughness. Although he had no diplomatic credentials, he negotiated an agreement with Greek shipowners about trade with Communist China. He conducted a search for spies in the Signal Corps and the Fort Monmouth laboratories. In these highly publicized enterprises he had the volunteered assistance of un-identified employees in the federal agencies who violated their trusts by supplying him with information about their colleagues and superiors.

Eventually military and civilian officers of the Pentagon came to feel that he was intolerable, and they resisted further pressure from him and his staff. This resistance led to mutual charges and recrimi-nations, and a special Senate committee was appointed to investi-gate the truth of the contradictory allegations. The committee, how-ever, merely aired and did not settle the controversy. In August 1954, Senator Ralph Flanders of Vermont introduced a resolution to censure McCarthy for his conduct, to which Senator William Ful-bright of Arkansas added further charges, such as that McCarthy had shaken down the Lustron Corporation for $10,000 for a publica-tion on housing. The Senate did not act on the Flanders resolution immediately, but authorized the appointment of a bipartisan select committee to hold hearings on the charges. Majority Leader William Knowland selected Arthur Watkins of Utah, Frank Carlson of Kansas, and Francis Case of South Dakota, and Minority Leader Lyndon Johnson chose Edwin Johnson of Colorado, John Stennis of Missis-sippi, and Samuel J. Ervin, Jr. of North Carolina to serve on the committee. Senator Watkins was elected chairman and the committee heard testimony on August 31 and for two weeks thereafter on the several categories of offense of which McCarthy was accused. There was no television, and Chairman Watkins made it clear at the start that he would not tolerate diversions, abruptly recessing the hearings at one point after lecturing McCarthy on decorum, an act that drew from McCarthy the deathless line, "This is the most unheard-of thing I ever heard of."

The Watkins committee was stern and decorous in its procedures, but it was selectively indulgent in some of the judgments it reached on the merits. One series of charges accused McCarthy of contempt of the Gillette-Hennings Subcommittee of the Committee on Privi-leges and Elections which, in 1951, had looked into accusations against McCarthy brought by Senator Benton of Connecticut. The subcommittee called on McCarthy to discuss certain funds collected for anti-Communist activities which, it was alleged, had been diverted to personal uses. Instead of cooperating with the subcommittee, McCarthy abused its members, failed to appear before it at all, although called many times, and issued a press statement in which he said of one of its members, Senator Hendrickson of New Jersey, that he was "a living miracle in that he is without question the only man who has lived so long with neither brains nor guts." The Watkins committee did not think that this was a very nice thing to say and recommended censure. Nor did it condone McCarthy's telling Senators Hayden and Gillette that he thought the subcommittee was "guilty of stealing just as clearly as though the members engaged in picking the pockets of the taxpayers and turning the loot over to the Democratic National Committee."

The judgment of the Watkins committee was more compassionate about what was described in the civil service prose of the committee counsel as "incidents of encouragement of United States employees to violate the law and their oaths of office or Executive orders." McCarthy had repeatedly told two million federal employees that he felt it was "their duty to give us any information which they have about graft, corruption, communism, treason," and he had said that there "is no loyalty to a superior officer which can tower above and beyond their loyalty to their country." Uncounted but doubtless large numbers of federal employees responded to this invitation to administrative sabotage, and the staff of the Permanent Subcommittee became a confessional for informers. Firm information about subversion was certainly scarce in the quiet tips provided by McCarthy's underground. McCarthy's scythe never cut over a field that had not already been swept before. McCarthy's invitation to "violate the law" did, however, get him a great chaff of spiteful insinuation and malicious accusation by those who had lost arguments with superiors over policy, had lived in a rivalry of hateful tensions about rank and assignment, were likely to lose jobs because of administrative decisions, or who felt religious animosity, rancor over lost romance, or bitterness about conflicts of artistic opinion.

The morale of several agencies was impaired by suspicion of undermining, including sections of the State Department, but the Watkins committee let Senator McCarthy off with a soft impeachment, preferring instead to maintain the futile theoretical position that the Congress has and should have unlimited access to execu-

FIGURE 1. Senator McCarthy called to the witness stand to testify about the two-and-one-fourth-page FBI letter (which he holds). Left to right: Francis P. Carr, Senator McCarthy, and Roy Cohn. In background is Secretary of the Army Robert Stevens. (*Brown Brothers*)

tive information, an argument that no president has honored, beginning with George Washington. The committee also let McCarthy off on the charge that he had received and used classified information wrongfully taken from an executive department. The charge grew out of an incident in the Army-McCarthy hearings when McCarthy produced a two-and-one-fourth-page paper purporting to be a letter from J. Edgar Hoover to Major General Bolling, Assistant Chief of Staff, G-2, about security arrangements at the Fort Monmouth Laboratory. Mr. Hoover said that there was no such letter, but that information in the doctored fake had been lifted from a fifteen-page memorandum from the FBI to Army Intelligence. McCarthy offered the forgery to the Mundt subcommittee which discreetly placed its contents beyond public discussion. Although it was a possible violation of espionage laws for McCarthy to have had a false document containing real information bearing on security, the Watkins committee found that he had been "under the stress or strain of being tried or investigated by the subcommittee," and that this was a mitigating circumstance.

The Watkins committee also condoned McCarthy's abuse of Senator Ralph Flanders of Vermont, although it had found that his abuse of Senator Hendrickson was censurable. There was, the committee thought, a difference between the circumstances in the two cases. On June 11, 1954, Senator Flanders had walked into the Senate caucus room where McCarthy was testifying coast to coast on television in the Army-McCarthy hearings, and had informed him that he was about to attack the junior senator from Wisconsin on the floor of the Senate. The appearance of Flanders had in fact been a little startling. After the incident, McCarthy was asked by the press to make a statement about the intended speech, and he said, "Senile—I think they should get a man with a net and take him to a good quiet place." Although the Watkins committee thought that McCarthy's crack about Flanders was vulgar and base, it was not censurable because Flanders had been provocative both in the caucus room and in speeches about McCarthy on the Senate floor.

The Watkins committee was tougher on McCarthy for his treatment of General Ralph W. Zwicker, who had been a witness in McCarthy's investigation of security at Fort Monmouth in February 1954. The immediate issue was military responsibility for the promotion of Captain Irving Peress to the rank of major and his honorable separation from the Army after he had taken the Fifth Amendment in earlier proceedings before McCarthy's subcommittee. McCarthy accused General Zwicker of arrogance, evasiveness, and contempt, and told him that he was both unfit to wear the uniform and that he should be removed from command. The committee recommended that McCarthy be censured for his treatment of General Zwicker.

It also recommended that he be censured for contempt of a Senate committee, but the debate on the recommendations and on Senator Flanders' original motion to censure was put off until after the November elections so as to permit the Senate, in the words of Knowland of California, to act "in an atmosphere free from pre-election tensions." Knowland moved to have the Senate consider the resolution of censure on November 10, and McCarthy's friends, both in and out of the Senate, moved to his defense. John Marshall Butler of Maryland thought that censure for pushing General Zwicker around would play into the hands of Communist lawyers who would goad the chairmen of investigating committees into further acts of censurable folly. Senator John Bricker of Ohio urged the view that McCarthy had merely shown "patriotic exuberance." Senator Barry Goldwater charged that the anti-McCarthy drive had been inspired by Communists who had cunningly shifted the leadership of the action to others. William Jenner of Indiana conceded that although individual senators were not disloyal, the censure proceeding itself was an aspect of the Communist conspiracy, the whole evidently being greater than the sum of its parts.

As the debate moved on, an organization headed by Lieutenant General George Stratemeyer, called "Ten Million Americans Mobilizing for Justice," launched a drive for ten million signatures to urge rejection of the censure resolution. The theory of the "Ten Million" was that the "Communists and their un-American cohorts, by vicious propaganda, and through willing stooges and blind but innocent dupes," had "victimized certain members of the U.S. Senate," and that Communist influence was responsible for both the Watkins committee and its recommendations. McCarthy distributed excerpts from the *Daily Worker* to all members of the Senate to show that the Communist party backed his censure. He later put material into the *Congressional Record* in which he blamed Communists for his plight in that they had made the Watkins committee an "unwitting handmaiden" and an "involuntary agent" of his ruin. He said that the whole censure proceeding was a "lynch bee" and that the Watkins committee had imitated Communist methods.

On December 2, 1954, the Senate voted to "condemn" McCarthy for contempt of the elections subcommittee, abuse of its members, and insults to the Senate during the censure proceedings themselves. There was no censure for McCarthy's treatment of General Zwicker. All forty-four Democrats and Wayne Morse, then an Independent, voted for the condemnation, and the Republicans split evenly. The final vote was sixty-seven to twenty-two.

From 1950 to 1954, the activities of Senator McCarthy were an oppressive weight and pain to tens of thousands in government, politics, and the professions specifically, and within the articulate and better-educated circles of society generally. In America and abroad he became a symbol of mortal danger to liberal values and democratic processes. Some of the distaste for him was undoubtedly aesthetic—in his official role, he was often loutish and saturnine, heavy and graceless, contemptuous and tough. But other political figures have been coarse and overbearing, without exciting the anxiety that McCarthy generated among so many. Was there something significantly different about McCarthy and his activities, something to make him politically ominous, a suggestion of fearful disruption just beneath the surface of the society?

He ceased to be an influential figure after his condemnation by the United States Senate for conduct unbecoming to his office. It would be easy to conclude from this that McCarthyism then was merely a flash of stunning but temporary impact associated with a demagogue of "brute brilliance," and that McCarthyism was nothing without McCarthy. But there is a considerable body of speculation that suggests that there is more to it than this, that McCarthyism was the surface appearance of serious strains in the social and political system. The readings that follow supply examples of the principal explanations of the meaning of McCarthyism.

One interpretation sees McCarthy primarily as a demagogue, and Luthin's version of this view is placed first among the essays because it also sets out the narrative of McCarthy's career. There are other variations of the theme of McCarthy as demagogue, one of which argues that McCarthyism was the logical fulfillment of a political style made popular by Franklin Roosevelt—direct appeals to the people against their elected representatives—the difference being that Roosevelt, like Pericles, was a gentleman, and McCarthy, like Cleon, was not.

A second interpretation considers McCarthyism to have been incipient totalitarianism, and an account of this conception is supplied by Dennis Wrong. From this category of opinions should be excluded those that carelessly use words like "totalitarian" and "authoritarian" as part of the rhetoric of dissent without suggesting an identity of philosophy and program. However, there are writers who have thought that although McCarthy had no program comparable with that of the dictators of Europe, the pattern of McCarthy's behavior was totalitarian in psychology and gesture (Marya Mannes); or that authoritarianism was the psychological characteristic of many of

McCarthy's followers (Richard Hofstadter); or that McCarthyism was even a species of American Fascism fostered by rightist elements (Carey McWilliams).

Conservative commentators have seen McCarthy and his works in a somewhat different light. They have tended to argue that McCarthy did a brave service in pressing investigations into Communist activity in the United States and that what was called "McCarthyism" was an invention of those who did not want to see communism exposed, attacked, and uprooted—that it was an organized slander by people willing to tolerate subversive evil. One conservative statement is the contribution by William Buckley, who argues that there is an orthodoxy of outlook on fundamentals in every society (including, therefore, democratic societies), that anticommunism is the American orthodoxy, and that McCarthyism was simply a hardening of that orthodoxy. The most sophisticated of the conservative evaluations is that of Willmoore Kendall who argues that what is called "McCarthyism" is not the real issue that divided people in the 1950s. It was the symptom, rather, of a graver although largely unclarified choice of courses which every free nation had to make in the late 1930s, namely, whether totalitarian movements would be permitted to emerge in their midst. The American consensus rejected them all—Nazi, Fascist, and Communist. Anti-McCarthyites were unwilling to accept this interpretation of the consensus, and "got mad" at McCarthyites for asserting that it was true.

One fashionable explanation of McCarthy puts him in the American Populist tradition, along with Pitchfork Ben Tillman and Sockless Jerry Simpson, and Leslie Fiedler's essay is one of several to make the suggestion. An established historian, C. Vann Woodward, however, has some words of qualification about certain prevailing conceptions of what the Populist heritage really is. Two views suggest that the central meaning of McCarthyism is sociological, that it was a product of status politics and new social anxieties (according to Daniel Bell) or of social strain (according to Talcott Parsons). All three of these interpretations—the historical, and the two sociological explanations—tend to overlap and to borrow from each other, but the centers are separate, however much the circumferences intersect.

One of the authors in the collection (Nelson Polsby) finds shortcomings in all three of these interpretations and suggests that

McCarthyism was a kind of grass-roots Republicanism, as local election results are said to demonstrate. What is the effect upon this interpretation (if any) of the fact that the proceedings that led to the condemnation of McCarthy by the Senate were started by a Republican senator, that it was a Republican Senate that voted the condemnation, and that the final vote was bipartisan, with 22 Repubicans voting against and with 44 Democrats and 22 Republicans voting for condemnation?

The collection of essays ends with a favorable summary of McCarthy's activities by Harold Lord Varney and an unfavorable summary by Richard Rovere. It is for every student of McCarthy and his times to judge for himself whether McCarthyism was an expression of irrationalism and frustration in the American society, or a justifiable response to a genuine threat to the national security.

I McCARTHY AS DEMAGOGUE

Reinhard H. Luthin

THE MAKING OF McCARTHY

Reinhard Luthin, a former member of the history faculty at Columbia University and Fulbright Professor of American and European History at the University of Dacca, Pakistan, was the author of works on Lincoln and of numerous articles in scholarly journals on aspects of American history. The book from which the following material was selected contains ten studies of political figures in the twentieth century.

Joseph R. McCarthy was born in Grand Chute, a quiet Wisconsin township, on November 14, 1909, to an Irish-American couple, Timothy and Bridget McCarthy. His early life was a pattern of insecurity and frustration, a piecemeal education, part-time farming, and a job as a grocery manager. With a high school diploma, won at the age of twenty-one after one year of schooling, McCarthy entered Marquette University, Milwaukee's Jesuit college. In 1935, he was graduated from Marquette's law school and practiced law for a year in Waupaca, Wisconsin. At this point a shrewd Republican party leader, Mike Eberlein, gave McCarthy a job in his law office; the fledgling politician began to get the laudatory headlines which were to smooth his path from Wisconsin to Washington, D.C.

The Shawano County *Journal* announced in February 1936 the arrival of "Jos. McCarthy," a young man with "a very creditable record of achievement." Within five months, McCarthy decided to become a Democratic politician. He was elected president of the Young Democratic Clubs of the Seventh Congressional District, and he announced his candidacy for District Attorney of Shawano County. (This was the year Franklin D. Roosevelt defeated Alfred M. Landon by a landslide vote. One wonders whether Republican Joseph McCarthy in 1954 remembers his appearance on a Democratic ticket during the period of Democratic rule which he later called "twenty years of treason.")

McCarthy did not win in his trial run as a Democrat. The Democrats were poorly organized, and they had to compete with the Progressive party, led by the La Follette brothers, as well as the

Republican party. For four decades the La Follette name, borne by
the Senators Robert M. La Follette, father and son, and Governor
Philip F. La Follette, had been a synonym for Wisconsin. For the
rest of the country the name suggested progressive, adventurous
government. By the late 1930s conservative Republicans began to
gain power in the state. In 1938 they won a decisive victory for
Senator Alexander Wiley, defeated Phil La Follette for governor, and
elected eight Republicans to Congress. By 1939, Wisconsin's political
future seemed to be in Republican hands. Perhaps this was Joseph
McCarthy's reason for leaving Democratic ranks and joining the
Republican party.

McCarthy's first venture as a Republican was his 1939 campaign
for circuit judge of the Tenth Judicial District. He advertised his
availability in the county papers and conducted a door-to-door can-
vass, asking homely questions of his prospective constituents, based
on information about their lives and problems picked up from their
neighbors. Like Huey Long in the rural North Louisiana parishes,
Joe McCarthy recognized a primary secret of successful politics—
that people will vote for a man who seems to care about them. He
won the election and began his judicial career on January 1,
1940. . . .

As a judge, McCarthy evinced a remarkable scorn for the law.
His conduct of one memorable case resulted in a severe rebuke by
the Wisconsin Supreme Court. In 1941, McCarthy dismissed a Wisconsin Department of Agriculture petition to force the Appleton
Quaker Dairy Company to abide by the state milk marketing law.
He also destroyed the notes of his statement dismissing the case on
the ground that "they weren't material." (It seems he had a friend
interested in the dairy's case.) The State Supreme Court called his
action "an abuse of judicial power," adding that "ordering destruction of these notes was highly improper. . . . The destruction of
evidence under these circumstances could only be open to the
inference that the evidence destroyed contained statements of fact
contrary to the position taken by the person destroying the evidence."

This scorn for the processes of law and disregard of evidence
established a pattern that was to become much clearer in McCarthy's
subsequent career.

In 1942, without resigning his judgeship, McCarthy joined the

Marines as a lieutenant. He served for two years as an intelligence officer in the Pacific Theater. (In later political campaigning he was to bill himself as a "tail-gunner.") His military career was rather ordinary and uneventful.

In 1944, he decided to give up combat with the Japanese in the Pacific and returned to combat Senator Alexander Wiley in the Wisconsin Republican primary. Wisconsin's Republican secretary of state, Fred Zimmerman, protested vainly to the state attorney general that it was unconstitutional for McCarthy to campaign for a nonjudicial office while he was still a judge. In any event, the Marine uniform which he wore during the campaign was not enough to ensure victory. He lost the primary election to Senator Wiley by some 74,000 votes out of 290,000 cast.

The following year, five months before the Japanese surrender, McCarthy resigned from the Marines and won reelection as a county judge. He began immediately to draw up the blueprint for a bigger battle—his fight to defeat Wisconsin's other senator, Robert M. La Follette, Jr., in 1946.

Judge McCarthy had chosen an opportune year to run against La Follette, for the senator's political fortunes were steadily ebbing after twenty-one years in Washington. . . .

La Follette's ultimate defeat in the primary election was compounded of many factors. The first was the declining fortune of the Progressive forces in the state. Secondly, La Follette spent less than $4,000 in the campaign, compared to the $50,000 spent in McCarthy's behalf. And La Follette, preoccupied with national and international issues in Washington and perhaps too confident of his home support, spent only one week campaigning in Wisconsin. His pre-Pearl Harbor isolationism had weakened his political reputation; his party switch annoyed many voters; and the national political trend was moving slowly in the direction of a more conservative Republican rule.

McCarthy exploited several issues which weakened La Follette at the polls. He stressed his Marine record; he charged that La Follette was afraid to explain his Senate votes on European questions to Wisconsin's Poles, Greeks, and Germans; he insinuated that La Follette was being used as a dupe by the Communists. Actually, the senator had been an outspoken anti-Communist for more than twenty years. Indeed, on May 31, 1945 he had delivered a three-hour speech on the Senate floor, analyzing the aggressive designs of the Soviet Union.

A few days after this speech, the Communists launched a counterattack which they maintained for a year and a half and which was to cost La Follette many votes. In those years the Communists controlled the Wisconsin organization of the CIO, and they mercilessly assailed La Follette, deliberately distorting his prolabor Senate record in an attempt to alienate trade-union voters. The CIO never criticized McCarthy. And thousands of union members forsook La Follette in his hitherto loyal labor bailiwicks—Milwaukee, Kenosha, and Racine—and voted instead in the Democratic primary.

At the general election, McCarthy faced Professor Howard McMurray of the University of Wisconsin as his Democratic opponent. McMurray proved to be a weak candidate. He was a Democrat in a Republican state, and many rural citizens were suspicious of college professors. It was a year of Republican victories throughout the North, and McCarthy received 620,430 votes to McMurray's 378,772.

McCarthy had encouraged the rural suspicions of McMurray ("I'm just a farm boy, not a professor," he told farmers). Perhaps his realization of the political potency, in some quarters, of an attack on colleges and intellectuals encouraged his increasing public contempt for universities and educated men generally.

McCarthy reached Washington in December of 1946. He had been in the capital only a few days when he called a press conference. This in itself was unusual for a freshman senator, but what he said was even more unusual. He had a solution for ending the coal strike: "Draft John L. Lewis [United Mine Workers chieftain] into the armed forces. Lewis should be directed to order the miners to mine coal. If he does not do that, he should be courtmartialed. We should go straight down the line. All this talk about you can't put 400,000 miners in jail is a lot of stuff." The new senator had apparently forgotten his primary campaign, when he scored President Truman's supposed "vicious anti-labor" policy and promised protection to trade unionists.

This peculiar conception of service in the United States Army as a form of punishment presaged a long series of assaults on the Army that was to characterize the senator's subsequent political career. This pattern of attack emerged again in 1949 when McCarthy charged that the Army had brutalized a group of Nazi SS officers who had been found guilty of shooting captured American troops during the Battle of the Bulge (1944). The attack was sharpened in 1951 and 1952 with his charges that General of the Army George C. Marshall had consistently served the interests of the Soviet Union. And in 1953 and 1954 McCarthy renewed his attack by accusing the Army of "coddling" Communists, a charge that culminated in the dramatic televised hearings conducted by the special Senate Subcommittee on Investigations. During these hearings, McCarthy's conception of Army service as a form of punishment reappeared in his charge that the Army had drafted his aide, G. David Schine, as a "hostage" to prevent further McCarthy committee investigation of the Army.

Soon after McCarthy's term began, 128 members of Washington's Press Gallery voted him the "worst" senator of the 96 in the Upper House. McCarthy tried hard, though, to be popular. He bought himself a tuxedo and made himself available to Washington society. He discarded his "sunburst" neckties for conservative cravats, and changed to dark suits, usually double-breasted. He was considered an "eligible bachelor" and was seen at cocktail and dinner parties.

During his first three years in the Senate, until 1950, McCarthy was a relatively obscure party man, not taken into high policy councils but faithful enough in the usual interparty struggles. His chief distinction was as the advocate of certain special interests. In conjunction with a campaign by the Pepsi-Cola Company, he moved to end the rationing of sugar. Similarly, he fought to block government-subsidized housing, and in 1948 accepted a fee of $10,000 from the Lustron Corporation, a manufacturer of prefabricated houses, for a pamphlet recommending government aid to prefab manufacturers. (The propriety of this action was questioned by a special Senate investigating subcommittee, since McCarthy was at the time a member of the Banking and Currency Committee, whose jurisdiction included the Federal housing agencies and the Reconstruction Finance Corporation to which Lustron owed $37 million, never repaid.)

McCarthy's record produced no enthusiasm and some formidable opposition in Wisconsin. Early in 1950, when McCarthy started to plan for his 1952 reelection campaign, he found little reassurance of strong support at home. The state's two most distinguished and widely-read newspapers, the Milwaukee *Journal* and the Madison

Capital-Times, had already begun to expose the most discreditable incidents of his judicial and senatorial career. Wisconsin aspirants to his Senate seat were certain of victory in 1952. The senator desperately needed an effective campaign issue. And with a sure instinct for the popular mood, he chose one that became a successful political rallying cry, a potent weapon in the struggle for power—the issue of "Communists in government."

McCarthy's first opportunity to exploit this issue came when the Ohio County Republican Women's Club of Wheeling, West Virginia, invited him to give a Lincoln Day oration on February 9, 1950.

The *Wheeling Intelligencer,* as reported by Frank Desmond of its staff, quoted McCarthy as saying with outraged indignation: "While I cannot take the time to name all of the men in the State Department who have been named as members of the Communist Party and members of a spy ring, I have here in my hand a list of 205 that were known to the Secretary of State as being members of the Communist Party and who, nevertheless, are still working and shaping the policy in the State Department." Those words, sent out by Associated Press, were printed in newspapers throughout the nation.

McCarthy continued westward. At Denver, Colorado, he substituted "205 bad risks" for the 205 "members of the Communist Party and of a spy ring." At Salt Lake City, Utah, he slashed the figure to 57. But as if to make up for the shrinkage in size, he now referred to the "57" as "card-carrying" Communists.

In Washington, McCarthy was challenged by John E. Peurifoy, deputy undersecretary of state, to name the "57 card-carrying Communists." "If you have this information," wrote Peurifoy, "as a loyal American you owe it to your country to inform the officials responsible. The thousands of loyal employees of this department must not be placed under a cloud of suspicion."

The senator did not name the 57—or even one. Instead, he released to the press a copy of a letter which he had sent to President Truman, in which he wrote:

While the records are not available to me, I know absolutely that of one group of approximately 300 certified to the Secretary for discharge, he actually discharged only approximately 80. . . . I would suggest therefore, Mr. President, that you simply pick up your phone and ask Mr. Acheson how many of those whom your [loyalty] board had labeled as dangerous he failed to discharge.

McCarthy's charges were greeted with skepticism by large sections of the press and the public, although many thousands accepted their authenticity. McCarthy's severe critic, the Milwaukee *Journal,* on February 14 (1950) challenged: "We suspect very much that his weekend oratorical spree is cut of demagogic cloth. It is up to the Senator to prove that it is not." On the following day President Truman publicly pronounced McCarthy a mishandler of the truth. The *New York Times* of February 22 commented: "Senator McCarthy has been giving a good imitation of a hit-and-run driver in his attacks on the State Department."

Suddenly McCarthy had a new number—this time, 81—which he was to use in the following weeks. He disposed of the "57" by explaining to the Senate: "Then, when I sent him [Truman] a telegram and said, 'Mr. President, I have the 57 names; they are yours if you want them'; and when he answered by calling me a liar, I felt I could get no cooperation from the President." The record would show that there were "81" involved, he insisted. To those who demanded why he did not turn over their names to the State Department, he answered: "Everything I have here is from the State Department's own files." But he would not divulge any names.

The nationwide furor that resulted from these charges led the Senate to create a special subcommittee of the Foreign Relations Committee to inquire into subversive activities, past and present, in the State Department. The subcommittee, headed by Senator Millard E. Tydings of Maryland, began its deliberations on March 8, 1950. Four months later the Democratic majority and the Republican minority issued separate reports of their conclusions. . . .

The Tydings committee majority report concluded that McCarthy's charges were "a fraud and a hoax." Therein it performed a disservice to the nation. For despite the fact that McCarthy had failed to turn up one Communist still employed in the State Department, despite his evasions and exaggerations, he had pointed out, as had others before him, the lax security procedures in the department. McCarthy was neither serious nor responsible in leveling his charges. Had the Tydings committee been less partisan and more serious, it would have discovered, as did others before and after it, that the State Department had been derelict in pursuing a vigorous and proper security policy in a number of cases presented to the committee by McCarthy.

"Joe—Yoo Hoo—Joe"

FIGURE 2. From *The Herblock Book* (Beacon Press, 1952).

But the failure of the Tydings committee to investigate properly was understandable, if not excusable, in view of the considerable skepticism that greeted McCarthy's largely unsubstantiated charges in many parts of the country and in the press. Senator McCarthy had never been one to quail before lack of evidence; to him the charge itself was often adequate proof; and the more sensational the charge, the better it suited his purpose.

McCarthy did not confine his political "circus," as *Commonweal,* a leading Catholic weekly, called it, to Washington. He took his anti-Red show on the road. He went on the radio and television and made personal appearances at gatherings of all sorts throughout the country. The senator made good "copy" with his sensational charges, and invariably reporters and photographers were on hand to supply that copy to their papers. McCarthy began to acquire a national following numbering into the millions.

Popular acceptance of McCarthy's anti-Communist campaign becomes understandable in the light of the developments that followed from the breakdown of America's wartime alliance with the Soviet Union and the cold war that ensued. . . .

The Soviet repudiation of the "Grand Alliance" and the outbreak of the cold war initiated a long, tedious, and often painful process of public education concerning the true nature of the Communist conspiracy and its effective penetration of government and private institutions. The revelation by Igor Gouzenko that a Soviet atom spy ring, with branches in Great Britain, Canada, and the United States, had successfully stolen and handed over to Moscow American atom bomb secrets shocked and frightened the American public. Further revelations by Communist defectors like Whittaker Chambers and Elizabeth Bentley documented the extent of Communist infiltration of the government. Congressional investigations in the late 1940s, led by both Democrats and Republicans, helped to enlighten the public and to spur the Truman administration to adopt a more stringent security program. The subsequent prosecution and conviction of Alger Hiss, Judith Coplon, William Remington, Julius and Ethel Rosenberg, and eleven American Communist leaders—all occurring during a period of heightened international tensions—not only awakened the public to the real dangers of Communist infiltration but made the people receptive to virtually any public charges of subversion. Although McCarthy had had nothing to do with the uncovering, prosecution, or conviction of any Communist spy or infiltrator, he shrewdly sensed the mood of the people and capitalized on it.

From the time of his Wheeling speech in February 1950, Senator McCarthy was in the process of winning his gamble to secure re-election in 1952. Certain widely circulated newspapers, like Colonel Robert R. McCormick's Chicago *Tribune* and Washington *Times-Herald,* and some popular columnists and radio commentators like George Sokolsky, Westbrook Pegler, Fulton Lewis, Jr., and Walter Winchell, did a great deal to popularize the Senator and to lend credence to the myth he so carefully nurtured—that he was responsible for cleaning the Reds out of government.

The first test of the efficacy of McCarthy's chosen instrument of power politics came in the fall of 1950 when his staff aided in the campaign that defeated his enemy, Senator Tydings, in the Maryland senatorial race. This campaign featured a technique that was to become a characteristic of McCarthy's political activity—the doctored document. In this case, the anti-Tydings forces produced a fake composite photograph showing the conservative Tydings in apparently friendly conversation with Earl Browder, the Communist leader. Not only was the photograph a fake, but the insinuation of pro-communism on Tydings' part was completely false. The Communists had continually denounced Tydings as a reactionary, and Tydings himself had once had Earl Browder cited for contempt of the Senate.

Tydings lost to his Republican opponent, John Marshall Butler. In February 1951, the Senate set up a special subcommittee to investigate the Maryland election. In August the committee reported that there was insufficient evidence to unseat Butler; but it denounced the tactics of the Butler forces as a "despicable 'back-street' type of campaign."

McCarthy claimed that "Communists-in-government" had been the big issue in the Maryland election, and his stock soared in the Republican party. This success spurred him on. In 1951, while continuing his assaults on the State Department, McCarthy began a campaign to vilify General of the Army George C. Marshall, then serving as secretary of defense. Marshall was vulnerable to a demagogic attack because of his role in the developments that ended in the Communist conquest of China.

In 1946 President Truman had sent Marshall as his special ambassador to mediate the conflict between Chiang Kai-shek's government and Mao Tse-tung's Communist rebels. The general felt himself blocked by the Kuomintang's obstruction and by the Communists' determination to wreck any peaceful settlement in order to win all of China. In January 1947, Marshall admitted the failure of his mission and returned to the United States. By 1949 the Communists had conquered the whole Chinese mainland.

The Marshall mission may have been ill-advised and inept; the whole China policy of the State Department may have been mistaken. But McCarthy sought to portray possible mistakes as virtual treason. In a three-hour speech on the Senate floor, on June 14, 1951, he developed the thesis that Marshall was implicated in a "great conspiracy" to aid the Soviet Union. His theme was that both Marshall and Dean Acheson were ready to sacrifice America's interests in order to advance Soviet power.

Several months later, the leading Senate Republican, Robert A. Taft, expressed disapproval of McCarthy's charges: "His extreme attack against General Marshall is one of the things on which I cannot agree with McCarthy. I think some criticism of General Marshall was justified, but he should not have been accused of affiliation with any form of Communism."

The following year, Republican presidential candidate Dwight D. Eisenhower was to eschew even the kind of criticism of McCarthy that Senator Taft had indulged in. In his campaign stops in Wisconsin, Eisenhower agreed to delete from his prepared speeches a passage of praise for General Marshall, his old friend and mentor. This decision was taken on political grounds, in the belief that McCarthy was a potent electoral asset to the Republican party and should not be alienated.

In view of this decision, it is instructive to analyze Senator McCarthy's record as a vote-getter for himself and for others.

The Baltimore *Sun,* Maryland's leading newspaper, pointed out in 1950 that McCarthy could by no means take all the credit for the Tydings defeat. The paper listed other important factors: Tydings' support of the Taft-Hartley Act, which alienated labor votes; his chairmanship of the Senate Armed Services Committee, which focused on himself some of the popular resentments against United States involvement in the Korean War; his heavy official duties in Washington, which made it impossible for him to conduct a sustained personal campaign in Maryland; a split in the Maryland Democratic party, which affected his political forces. The *Sun* also pointed out that Tydings ran thousands of votes ahead of all other candidates on the Democratic ticket in Maryland. Denounced by Mc-Carthy, he nevertheless outdistanced at the polls those Democrats about whom McCarthy was silent.

What of McCarthy's more extensive campaigning in 1952, the year General Eisenhower won a great electoral victory and swept many lesser Republicans into office on his coattails? The senator's record that year was spotty. His chief victim was Senator William Benton, who was running for reelection in Connecticut.

In 1951, Benton had introduced a resolution in the Senate to impeach McCarthy. Benton's resolution listed many particulars, including charges of financial irregularities, perjured testimony before the Tydings committee, and attempted deceptions of the Senate in his attacks on General Marshall and others. A special Senate Rules Subcommittee was set up to determine whether Benton's charges warranted the expulsion of McCarthy. (A year and a half later, the subcommittee issued a report in which it made no findings, but raised six leading questions about McCarthy's career. It failed to supply direct answers to its questions, but the implications were unmistakable.)

In 1952, McCarthy carried the fight to Benton. He challenged his avowed enemy to repeat his charges without benefit of congressional immunity—something that McCarthy himself had repeatedly failed to do. Benton repeated the charges on a radio broadcast, and McCarthy sued him for libel. This was clearly a move in his campaign to defeat Benton in Connecticut's senatorial race. (In 1954, McCarthy withdrew his libel suit, on the pretext that he had found no one who believed the Benton charges, whereupon thousands of citizens from every part of the country wrote, wired, and telephoned statements expressing their belief in the charges.)

Benton was defeated in his reelection campaign, but here too McCarthy cannot be given full credit, for the Eisenhower victory helped the Republicans to take over most of Connecticut's state and federal offices.

On the other hand, despite the Eisenhower sweep, McCarthy's personal campaigning failed to reelect Senator James P. Kem of Missouri and Senator Harry Cain of Washington. The inefficacy of

McCarthy's help is underscored by the fact that in these two cases, he was campaigning *for* friends rather than *against* enemies.

And in his own reelection campaign in Wisconsin, McCarthy hardly emerged as the popular hero he had expected to be on the basis of his three-year buildup as America's Number One Anti-Communist.

McCarthy's primary and general election campaigns were amply financed. The McCarthy Club of Milwaukee, the largest group supporting him, spent more than $160,000. The Republican Voluntary Committee used large sums also. In addition, sizeable contributions were obtained from some of the senator's wealthy backers, such as Hugh R. Cullen, the Texas oil millionaire, and Frederick C. Miller, a Milwaukee brewer.

Eisenhower beat Stevenson in the Badger State by more than 357,000 votes. Republican Governor Walter Kohler defeated his Democratic opponent by more than 400,000. The margin of victory for the G.O.P. candidates for lieutenant-governor, state treasurer, and attorney general exceeded 425,000 for each. Pointedly enough, Fred R. Zimmerman, the Republican secretary of state, publicly and privately a strong anti-McCarthy man, emerged as top man on the Wisconsin state ticket. Zimmerman received a staggering plurality of one-half million votes over his Democratic rival.

And what was McCarthy's showing? The senator received 870,444 votes to 731,402 for his Democratic opponent—a plurality of less than 140,000. He was low man among all Republican candidates for major office in Wisconsin's state ballot. Some Wisconsinites concluded that Eisenhower himself would have done as well as the state candidates on his party's ticket if he had not been prevailed upon to endorse McCarthy for reelection.

During the 1952 campaign it was predicted that if the Republicans won, a "new McCarthy" would emerge. His attacks on the State Department would cease with the retirement of Secretary Acheson and the whole Democratic administration, and McCarthy, as a member of the majority party, would play fairly on the new President's team. . . .

When the Republican-controlled Congress was organized in January 1953, McCarthy was given choice committee assignments, particularly the chairmanship of the Government Operations Committee and its Permanent Subcommittee on Investigations. Heretofore, the function of these two groups had been to serve as "watchdog" over the efficiency and honesty of government operations; the Senate Internal Security Subcommittee, headed by Senator Pat McCarran, Nevada, and then by Senator William Jenner, Indiana, had been responsible for investigating Communist infiltration and subversion. McCarthy immediately transformed the functions of his own committee and began to poach on Jenner's Communist-hunting preserve.

McCarthy's career as an inquisitor began in earnest in February 1953, just three weeks after the Eisenhower inauguration. He launched an investigation into alleged Communist subversion of the government's anti-Communist propaganda agency, the International Information Administration (whose overseas radio broadcasting arm was the Voice of America). With his powers of subpoena, he called on the carpet scores of men allegedly involved in the Communist conspiracy. Two of the most sensational cases in this investigation involved Reed Harris, deputy chief of the information program, and James Wechsler, editor of the *New York Post.*

Harris was given a severe grilling about his alleged leftist connections at Columbia University back in 1932 and his authorship, during the same period, of a book attacking commercialism in college football. But McCarthy failed to advance even one shred of evidence connecting Harris with communism. The senator's purposes had been served, however, by the opportunity this case gave him to publicize his sensational, if false, charges to a nationwide television audience.

Wechsler, once a member of the Young Communist League, but for more than fifteen years a vigorous anti-Communist, was questioned at an executive session of the subcommittee. McCarthy's pretext in calling Wechsler was that some of the editor's books had appeared on the shelves of the government's overseas libraries. But the books were never identified in the course of the hearing, and it became clear that the real reason for the inquisition was Wechsler's vigorous opposition to Senator McCarthy. . . .

Almost from the very beginning of his assumption of his committee chairmanship, McCarthy used his chosen instrument of power— the "Communists-in-government" issue—to bludgeon the Eisenhower administration just as he had used it against the Truman administration. By 1953, McCarthy, as ambitious as the late Senator Huey Long—whose presidential aspirations had led him into his abortive attempt to ruin the Democratic party—had no qualms about splitting the Republican party wide open to satisfy his insatiable hunger for power.

The Eisenhower administration, in a Job-like search for peace, went a long way toward appeasing him, but all to no avail. The president gave McCarthy his share of federal patronage. He overlooked and forgave many of McCarthy's attacks on the administration's policies and policy-makers. And although Eisenhower's patience gradually lessened, the president remained silent in a supreme effort to maintain party harmony and national unity.

McCarthy brought his attack on the Eisenhower administration into the open in March 1953 when he challenged the appointment of Charles Bohlen as U.S. ambassador to the Soviet Union. The Bohlen appointment was the immediate issue; but McCarthy boasted of his real aim to one Washington correspondent: "You wait, we're going to get Dulles' head."

John Foster Dulles, President Eisenhower's secretary of state, had inherited from his predecessor, Dean Acheson—along with some 42,000 employees and numerous big and little international problems —the thick fog of suspicion that hung over the Department of State. Dulles' task was to dispel that fog and to restore public and congressional confidence in the department. He sought to do this partly by avoiding conflict and cooperating with congressional investigators of subversive activities.

McCarthy provided Dulles with no disclosures of disloyalty in the State Department unearthed by his subcommittee, and he was to unearth precious few in the rest of the government during the succeeding months. Nor did he give the secretary of state a breathing spell to straighten matters out in the department. He plunged right in with a challenge to Eisenhower's appointment of Bohlen and with questions as to the veracity and integrity of Dulles, and even of Senators Robert A. Taft and William F. Knowland, who led the administration fight for Bohlen's confirmation. McCarthy's challenge was turned aside when the Senate approved the appointment, 74 to 13.

Almost immediately, McCarthy had another card to play against Dulles and Eisenhower—the so-called Greek Ships Agreement. The senator made what he called a "very important" announcement: he had made a "deal" with certain owners of Greek ships who promised to stop carrying cargoes to and from Red China. Actually, the State Department had concluded a similar agreement with the Greek government weeks before, and McCarthy knew it; his deal was nothing more than a play for sensational headlines.

Mutual Security Director Harold E. Stassen angrily issued a statement before the McCarthy subcommittee, charging that McCarthy was "undermining" the nation's foreign policy; that the sensational announcement of the McCarthy "deal" was "harmful" to America's efforts to negotiate by quiet diplomatic means an international accord with the free world to cut trade with Red China. Stassen argued heatedly that McCarthy had encroached on State Department functions, and he completely rejected the value of the whole "agreement."

The following day, President Eisenhower, in an obvious effort to maintain party harmony, virtually repudiated the Stassen statement, calling it merely Stassen's "opinion." And peace was finally restored at a luncheon between McCarthy and Dulles, during which a public statement was drafted reaffirming the executive's constitutional responsibility for the conduct of foreign relations but eliciting no promise from McCarthy to abstain from further encroachments. The senator had raked in some blue chips in his showdown with Dulles.

In April 1953, while the administration was trying to cement its relations with America's allies, McCarthy succeeded in substantially lowering this country's prestige abroad. This success was accomplished by the ten-day whirlwind trip his two chief aides, Roy M. Cohn and G. David Schine, made through Western Europe and England. They were ostensibly looking for waste, mismanagement, and subversion in the government's overseas libraries. These they failed to find, but their snooping shenanigans through the capitals of Europe, which cost the government over $8,000, made America an object of ridicule. The conservative *London Express* commented: "McCarthy is seeking to promote bitterness between Britain and America, thereby playing Malenkov's game."

McCarthy continued his direct assault on the administration during the summer of 1953 by conducting a vendetta against Dr. Robert L. Johnson, new head of the information agency, and by threatening an investigation of the Central Intelligence Agency, headed by Allen Dulles, brother of the secretary of state. Dr. Johnson resigned in June on grounds of "ill health." But McCarthy did not fare so well in his fight with the CIA. Here the administration held firm, and the senator was forced to back down.

McCarthy found his power severely challenged in July and August of 1953. He had become so arbitrary as subcommittee chairman that the three minority members, Democratic Senators McClellan, Symington, and Jackson, resigned in protest against McCarthy's insistence on his sole power to hire and fire subcommittee staff members. A storm of protest had arisen over his employment of J. B. Matthews as executive director of the subcommittee. Matthews had made reckless charges of Communist infiltration against large numbers of the Protestant clergy, and President Eisenhower himself joined in repudiating these charges. McCarthy was forced to accept Matthews' resignation. That summer, Richard H. Rovere, the *New Yorker's* Washington correspondent, reported that McCarthy was "confronted by the most acute crisis of his career."

By the fall, however, McCarthy was back.

In October, amidst a corps of reporters and news photographers, the senator and his attractive research assistant, Miss Jean Kerr, were married at a mass in St. Matthew's Cathedral in Washington, followed by a reception at the Maryland home of Colonel Bertie McCormick's niece. The senator was still on his West Indies wedding trip when he received word that the Army had suspended as "security risks" several civilian employees working on top-secret research materials at the Army Signal Center in Fort Monmouth, New Jersey. The patriotic bridegroom dramatically flew back to New York and began closed hearings.

Unidentified witnesses scuttled in and out of the hearing room; at regular intervals the senator would emerge to produce a sensational new charge or dark hint of Soviet espionage at Monmouth. Secretary of the Army Robert T. Stevens, who cooperated with the McCarthy investigation (in line with the Eisenhower policy of maintaining party harmony and working amicably with Congress), repeatedly stated that both the Army and the FBI had conducted lengthy inquiries into the security situation at Monmouth and had found no evidence of espionage or any other subversive activities.

The nation's press, meanwhile, played the story pretty much as McCarthy planned it. Even the sober *New York Times* had printed, on the basis of the senator's daily briefings on the closed hearings, such headlines as "Rosenberg Called Radar Spy Leader," "Radar Witness Breaks Down—Will Tell All About Spy Ring," "Monmouth Figure Linked To Hiss Ring." By January 1954, the *Times* realized it had been taken in by the McCarthy story, and it set the record straight in a three-article series by correspondent Peter Kihss.

Kihss concluded that McCarthy's investigation did not turn up anything new in security leaks or espionage, and had actually damaged the morale of scientists and other employees at Fort Monmouth. He reported: "The record is that the Army and the Eisenhower Administration had already tightened security regulations and opened investigations under the President's April 27 [1953] executive order before the McCarthy Inquiry turned toward Monmouth." Kihss conceded that the *Times* readers had been misled, and he added:

> For the newspapers, Fort Monmouth has been a lesson that will not quickly be forgotten, but the reading public should understand that it is difficult, if not impossible, to ignore charges by Senator McCarthy just because they are usually proved exaggerated or false. The remedy lies with the reader.

McCarthy's investigation at Monmouth represented another round in his continuing battle with the U.S. Army. It was also one more stage of his campaign against the Eisenhower administration. The high point of this campaign occurred in November 1953, as a result of a sensational accusation made by Attorney General Herbert Brownell against former President Truman. Brownell charged that Truman had appointed Harry Dexter White as assistant secretary of the treasury in 1947 despite several clear FBI warnings that White was a member of a Soviet espionage ring. The former president took to the air to deny the charge and to give his side of the story. But he unwittingly played directly into McCarthy's hands by denouncing the attorney general's motives in resurrecting the White case as an instance of "McCarthyism."

The senator immediately demanded, and received, free radio and television time to "answer" what he called Truman's attacks on him. McCarthy said considerably less about Truman and White over his nationwide hook-up on November 24, 1953, than he did about the Eisenhower administration. The "answer" to Truman turned into a diatribe on the Republican administration. McCarthy lamented that the administration had not done enough to fight communism, and he flatly opposed the president's expressed hope that "Communism-in-government" would not be an issue in the 1954 congressional elections.

The senator had a main issue of his own for 1954: himself. If the people believe in getting rid of subversives, he appealed, "then their answer is to keep the Republicans in power so we may continue to clean out the Augean stables." And he offered himself as the chief stable boy: "Democratic office-seekers," he told his audience, "have been proclaiming that McCarthyism is the issue in this campaign. In a way, I guess it is, because Republican control of the Senate determines whether I shall continue as chairman of the investigating committee." McCarthy also berated the administration for sending "perfumed notes" to our allies, "following the style of the Truman-Acheson regime," while doing nothing about the allies' trade with Red China. The senator advocated a "get tough" policy with our allies; a demand that they cut off their trade with Communist China or face the loss of American aid.

The White House was infuriated. McCarthy had declared himself, not the president's policies, the issue in the 1954 elections; he told his vast audience to vote Republican if they approved of him, Democratic if they disapproved. And he had made a slashing attack on the administration's handling of foreign policy.

Secretary Dulles, aroused by McCarthy's assault, spearheaded the administration's counterattack, with the president's approval. Dulles said: "We do not propose to throw away those precious assets [of mutual respect and friendship] by blustering and domineering methods." Other free nations, he continued, will be treated as "sovereign equals" and not as "our satellites." And the following day the president reiterated his support of Dulles.

But McCarthy continued on his way. He appealed to "every American who feels as I do about this blood trade with a mortal enemy to write or wire the President." The flow of letters and telegrams, pro and con, that went to Eisenhower must have been a keen disappointment to the senator. A total of less than 25,000 telegrams were received at the White House, scarcely an impressive figure compared with similar ones in the past. (President Roosevelt once received 3 million letters in three months during a March-of-Dimes campaign; passage of the Taft-Hartley labor-relations law produced some 25,000

messages daily; and President Truman's recall of General Mac-
Arthur from his Far Eastern command resulted in a flood of about
45,000 telegrams and letters, sent without any organized campaign.)

McCarthy was determined not to allow the Eisenhower administration to seize the Communists-in-government issue from him or to let
the president take it out of politics. But a surprise Democratic victory in a special congressional election called in a traditionally Republican Wisconsin district led him to seek another vote-garnering
issue. The Democratic victory had been interpreted as the result of
a protest vote against the Eisenhower farm policy, and so Joe Mc-
Carthy became an ardent advocate of 100 per cent fixed parity pay-
ments in opposition to the president's more flexible farm support
policy.

When the second session of the 83rd Congress convened in January 1954, McCarthy faced the necessity of requesting a new appropriation to keep his committee in operation. In such circumstances,
even the most ruthless of committee chairmen makes a show of
common politeness and good manners. McCarthy sounded a note of
repentance and compromise for his future dealings with both the
Democrats and the administration. On the basis of his promise of
procedural reform in running the committee, the three Democratic
members resumed their places on it. And this note of sweet reason-
ableness also seemed to imply that he would withdraw his fire from
the administration.

But almost immediately after the Senate voted overwhelmingly
(85 to 1) to renew his funds, the senator renewed his war upon
the Democrats and the administration. In a series of Lincoln Day
speeches, entitled "Twenty Years of Treason," he blasted the Democratic party as the party that had betrayed America's security and
vital interests to the Soviet enemy. With demagogic excess he
charged that those who wore the Democratic label "wear it with the
stain of a historic betrayal; wear it with the blood of dying men who
crawled up the hills of Korea while the politicians in the Democratic
Party wrote invitations to the Communists to join them in the United
Nations."

Simultaneously, McCarthy opened fire once more on the U.S.
Army. The Army had made the mistake of honorably discharging a
dentist who had been named before the McCarthy committee as a
Communist. On this basis, McCarthy accused the Army of "coddling

Communists." This charge led him into a direct conflict with Secretary of the Army Stevens. And this conflict ultimately led to the degrading spectacle, in the spring of 1954, of the nationally televised hearings in which a committee investigated its own chairman and staff and their relations with the civilian heads of the Army Department. These hearings were the culmination of the McCarthy assault on the Eisenhower administration.

II McCARTHYISM: INCIPIENT TOTALITARIANISM

Dennis H. Wrong

McCARTHYISM AS TOTALITARIANISM

Dennis Wrong, a Canadian scholar and social critic, is a member of the sociology faculty of New York University. He has taught at the New School for Social Research and was editor of Social Research, a publication of the New School.

There are signs that Senator McCarthy is slipping. One holds one's breath, for he has stormed back into the headlines to win new triumphs before. But whether he stays or goes it is important to define the social and political roots of "McCarthyism" to see how closely the "ism" is linked to the man. By now, one would expect to find many authoritative interpretations of the political tendency he personifies. Yet such are the passions McCarthy arouses that most discussions of him amount to little more than manifestoes of denunciation or documented exposés. The number of serious political analyses of the man, his mass support and the national mood he expresses, remains surprisingly small.

The very terms in which McCarthy is castigated imply certain "theories" about him. Those who view him primarily in the perspective of the American political tradition assimilate his career to that of other specimens of *demagogus Americanus*. Their verdict is that he is just another unscrupulous politician feeding on the tensions of the period, but destined to be repudiated and to descend into the limbo of "lunatic fringe" politics. Others, more impressed by analogies with recent European history, picture McCarthy as the leader of a formidable reactionary, even fascist, movement, enrolling new millionaires, segments of the Army and the Catholic Church, and an embittered small-town bourgeoisie in what will, it is predicted, remain a powerful faction in American politics for some time to come. A third view sees McCarthy as a mere incident in the slow drift toward the garrison state which started before his rise and will not be checked appreciably by his fall.

The most recent book-length study, *McCarthy and the Communists* by James Rorty and Moshe Dector, sticks fairly closely to the man

Dennis H. Wrong, "Theories of McCarthyism—A Survey," *Dissent* (Autumn 1954): 385–392. Reprinted by permission of the publisher.

and his public record. The book is essentially a "campaign document" meant to persuade that public which approves McCarthy's
"objectives" while deprecating his "methods," of the insincerity and
opportunism of his anti-Communism. The authors' documentation is
thorough and they make a few useful distinctions between the Mc-
Carthyites and organized totalitarian movements, but their book is
chiefly of interest as an expression of the embarrassment and irrita-
tion with which those intellectuals who have, as it were, enlisted for
the duration of the cold war confront McCarthy. Their main com-
plaints are that "he has never proved the seriousness and substan-
tiality of his anti-Communism" and that "both [his] tactics and
strategy can only be destructive of the ends sought by authentic
anti-Communists."

There is something profoundly disquieting about these terms of
opposition to McCarthy, particularly when one remembers that the
research for the book was supported by the American Committee for
Cultural Freedom. Rorty and Dector are evidently among those intellectuals so ready to serve as unofficial voices of America that they
can barely bring themselves to condemn McCarthyism in the large.
Their attacks must constantly be interlarded with denunciations of
the "anti-anti-Communists" and Europeans who exaggerate Mc-
Carthy's power or, like Alan Westin in the July *Commentary,* with
warnings that the Communists are exploiting the McCarthy issue.

It hardly needs to be said that the editors of the *Nation* and some
European neutralists turn out a good deal of undiscriminating cant
about "reigns of terror" in the United States, and certainly the remaining home-grown Stalinists are giving their own twist to anti-
McCarthyism. But that McCarthyism, whatever its origins or ultimate
significance, has created a national climate in which departures from
the most elementary decencies of a democratic society are imper-
ceptibly becoming the norm is something that these cold war cru-
saders cannot bring themselves to admit without all sorts of public
relations demurrers. In the end they reveal more about the limits of
their own concern over McCarthyism than about the phenomenon
itself.

Rorty and Dector might argue that *they* are deeply disturbed by
McCarthy's inroads on civil liberties, but that their intended audience
is less likely to be moved by the protests of civil libertarians than by
demonstrations of McCarthy's ineffectiveness as a Communist-hunter.

Apart from the questionable expediency and the even more doubtful morality of such a propagandistic approach, what disturbs one about too many of these intellectuals is the way in which their chosen public roles as spokesmen for the American intellectual community have completely usurped what should be their primary roles as critics of society and defenders of freedom.

Few serious analysts have pictured McCarthy as the leader of a fascist movement. The absence of an economic crisis, McCarthy's concentration on a single issue and his consequent failure to develop a broad political program and the unorganized character of his support, have frequently been noted as features clearly differentiating his following from the disciplined and ideologically self-conscious fascist movements which developed in Europe and America during the depression years. There are, however, a number of "class theories" of McCarthyism which have characterized it as at least an incipient fascist movement.

The familiar "Marxist" notion that the long-standing Taft-Dewey split in the Republican party reflects a division within "the ruling class" between eastern financial capital and midwestern industrial capital has been refurbished to explain the Eisenhower-McCarthy split, with McCarthy cast in the role of Taft's heir. The difference between Taft's fussy integrity and McCarthy's improvised hysterics is said to be the measure of the distance we have travelled toward "fascism." This view, which answers to the necessity felt by a certain kind of Marxist to find conflicts of economic interest behind all political struggles, has never had very much to recommend it. Midwestern industrial capital as represented by the leaders of General Motors and Chrysler conspicuously supported Eisenhower in 1952, and Taft himself shortly before his death criticized the big business composition of Eisenhower's cabinet and publicly reminded the president that there were many "middle class" Republican voters.

Undeniably McCarthy has inherited some of Taft's support, but if he has failed to put forward a social program that might attract radicalized masses in a depression he has equally failed to make himself, as Taft did, the spokesman of opposition to the welfare state. His voting record in Congress has become increasingly conservative, but there are many other Republican politicians who are more closely identified with the crabbed bourgeois conservatism that Taft epitomized. McCarthy's support among politicians comes largely from the ranks of these old Taftmen, but his mass following crosses party lines and he has been careful not to jeopardize its loyalty by making speeches on "the menace of creeping socialism." McCarthy's anti-intellectualism and antimilitarism, his stress on his plebeian origins and his sneers at gentility are even reminiscent of some strains of Populist oratory, although it is impossible to accept Leslie Fiedler's characterization of him in *Encounter* as simply a latter-day mid-western Populist.

A more sophisticated version of the "split in the ruling class" theory has been advanced by the editors of the Stalinoid journal *Monthly Review.* They see McCarthy as the candidate of the men of new wealth who have sprung up in the years of war and postwar prosperity. Plebeian, uncultured, often even uneducated and aggressive, resembling somewhat the robber barons of the last century, the Texas oil millionaires and their smaller-scale counterparts resent the political and social dominance of the wealthy old families of the eastern seaboard. Their lavish support of McCarthy represents an effort to attain national political power by ousting both the liberal Democrats and the Republican "sophisticated conservatives."

Clearly McCarthy has mobilized new wealth of this sort behind him. David Schine and William Buckley, second-generation heirs to fortunes made in the hotel business and the oil industry, are other conspicuous examples. The former a Jew and the latter a Catholic, both are outside the circle of established Protestant families. Buckley's book attacking the Yale faculty and his almost obsessive hatred of the "respectable" Ivy League intelligentsia are symptomatic.

The *Monthly Review* editors attribute McCarthy's failure to develop a demagogic social program which might win him support in the depression they anticipate, to a fear of alienating his reactionary backers. Their article appeared last January and they made much of McCarthy's silence during the recession and his failure to exploit the farm discontent rising in his home state. He has, however, since emerged, if somewhat belatedly, as an active proponent of higher fixed price supports than the present ones. Furthermore, the *Monthly Review* editors fail to note that McCarthy became a national figure before he attracted the support of new millionaires. One of his most novel characteristics is his ability to make use of the mass media: he is the first American politician to win a wide and fanatical following solely by calculated exploitation of the machinery of publicity. If the weight he is believed to carry with the electorate has encouraged rich men to finance him, there is nevertheless a sense in which they need him as much as he needs them.

The Texas oilmen have a definite but quite limited stake in national politics. They wanted a Republican president and Congress to give them rights to tidelands oil, and even the faintest suggestion of possible revision of the tax depletion allowances which have permitted them to keep their millions will loosen their bankrolls. But beyond this, they have no labor problem in an industry which employs little manpower and there is obviously no formidable party of the Left nor the prospect of one to challenge the sources of their wealth. If McCarthy votes for reactionary measures in Congress to please them, there are scores of other legislators who are more useful "waterboys for the vested interests" quietly rigging legislation in the lobbies and committees of Congress. The oilmen's support of McCarthy, as the *Monthly Review* editors seem to recognize, is less a matter of economic self-interest than a grandiose gesture expressing their uninhibited craving for additional power and prestige, as well as *arriviste* resentment of the mellowed wealth of the eastern "aristocracy." It is certainly doubtful that they would continue to back him if he became a gold brick reformer in the Huey Long pattern; however his power, like Hitler's in relation to the Ruhr industrialists, rests essentially on mass support so that he is far from being solely the instrument of the businessmen currently sponsoring him.

The fact that McCarthy's support comes from groups at both the top and bottom of the class hierarchy does give his following a certain similarity to that of the Nazis. But in the absence of severe internal crisis he cannot be classified as a full-fledged Fascist, for an economic depression or a catastrophe promoting comparable disintegration is the classic circumstance favoring a fascist movement. Most forebodings about McCarthy's prospects as an American Hitler have, consequently, stemmed from speculations on what his movement might become in the event of a depression. Could he re-adapt the Communist issue to appeal to a nation suffering from mass unemployment or could he successfully identify himself with a new program while retaining his present supporters? Both possibilities appear doubtful. Here we enter a highly speculative realm, but it now seems probably accurate to conclude as one observer has that "McCarthy is the luxury of a full-employment economy."

What large and stable elements in the American body politic has McCarthy successfully mobilized? To answer this question, full measure must be taken of McCarthy's ingenuity in single-mindedly concentrating on an issue which arises out of the troubled conditions of world politics but which he has adroitly transformed into a now bogus domestic issue: Communist infiltration of American society. Since the cold war is unlikely to disappear overnight, McCarthy has been able to exceed the life span of earlier nativist demagogues who achieved brief national prominence by playing on transitory economic dissatisfactions. It is the shadow of the cold war rather than the class war which has recently loomed largest in our politics.

This means that to discover the core of McCarthy's support, one must look for groups sharing a common outlook on foreign policy rather than on domestic economic questions. Samuel Lubell sketched the outlines of the McCarthyite coalition in *The Future of American Politics* and, following his lead, Nathan Glazer as advanced in an able article in *Commentary* what might be called, in contrast to the "class theories" discussed above, an "ethnic theory" of McCarthyism. Noting the thinly-concealed pro-Nazi position that McCarthy took in the 1948 Senate hearings on the Malmedy massacres, Glazer sees him as the heir of the old isolationist leaders whose most steadfast followers were of German and Irish descent. The revelations of Communist infiltration in the Roosevelt and Truman administrations gave these groups a chance to charge the leaders of the war with treason and thus retrospectively to justify their opposition to American participation.

In the 1930s and early 1940s these ethnic isolationists found sufficient numbers of *ad hoc* allies to become a powerful bloc capable of delaying active American resistance to the Axis powers. Some liberals and socialists with pacifist leanings, the Communists in the years of the Stalin-Hitler pact, Italian-Americans who sympathized with Mussolini, and businessmen who admired the European dictators' "solution" of the "labor problem" all joined in support of America First. In their current support of McCarthy the German and Irish blocs have found a new set of *ad hoc* allies: other ethnic groups, especially the Poles, whose homelands have been occupied by the

Soviet Union, fanatically anti-Communist religious groups, the new millionaires anxious to make a splash in national politics, and a substantial number of Americans, particularly among the less educated, who are baffled by the frustrations of the cold war and the failures of American foreign policy. And in both periods Republican politicians have actively tried to weld these heterogeneous groupings into a firm alliance against the Democrats.

It is the merit of Glazer's approach to show how the old ethnic isolationists have persisted in spite of their silence in the war and early postwar years and have now reappeared as the largest elements in McCarthy's mass following. At a time when foreign policy questions have once again become primary, they have regained much of their prewar power through their ability to swing votes across party lines. Yet Glazer observes that even at the height of their power the old isolationists were unable to elect a president or even to dictate the selection of a major party candidate. He concludes that the chances of McCarthy capturing the presidency are slight. His arguments are compelling, but the question of whether McCarthy could ever be elected president is altogether too narrow a compass in which to evaluate his role and prospects. Moreover, Glazer does not touch on the larger question of McCarthyism as a mood infecting even the senator's opponents.

Before considering the "ism" as something partially independent of the man, it is necessary to note another possible "road to power" which McCarthy as the leader of a fascist movement could conceivably follow. Since he leads a foreign policy rather than a class coalition, defeat in war might play the role for him that economic depression played for Hitler. Glazer qualifies his optimism with recognition of this possibility. The loss of India to the Communists, the complete collapse of NATO, another war like the Korean—might not defeats of this magnitude thoroughly discredit present American policy and further polarize public opinion to such an extent that the McCarthyites could develop into a genuine fascist movement with a chance of gaining power?

The essence of McCarthyism may be an assault on traditional liberties, but their erosion clearly started before McCarthy hit the headlines. It started in fact when the cold war began in earnest in 1946–47. Recognizing this, many interpreters have minimized the significance of McCarthy himself and seen him merely as the symbol of a drift towards militarized bureaucratic government in which civil liberties are given short shrift.

"War," Randolph Bourne once remarked, "is the health of the state." Civil liberties in America have suffered most during wars and immediately before or after them. The First World War witnessed the summary imprisonment of antiwar socialists and pacifists, and the persecution of German-Americans. The Smith Act was passed in 1940, a year before Pearl Harbor, and during the war the mass deportation of Japanese-Americans from the West Coast was one of the most flagrant violations of civil liberty in American history. It is neither surprising nor novel that the conflict with Russia should have produced similar occurrences. What is novel about the present situation is that, except for Korea, the conflict has been political and economic rather than military. European nations have long become accustomed to living in the shadow of war, but cold wars are a new experience to Americans. And the seeming endlessness of the cold war has created the mood of distemper and blocked aggression which has given McCarthy his opportunity.

Since the cold war will continue even if McCarthy suffers a political eclipse, he has served as a scapegoat for some "liberals" who by concentrating their fire on him have been able to avoid confronting the crimes committed or condoned by their friends. Yet, while less damaging to the cause of civil liberties, the opposite extreme of emphasizing McCarthyism without McCarthy also involves some distortion of reality. For McCarthy's activities have greatly accelerated the brutalization of our politics. The Smith Act convictions for words rather than deeds, the unprecedented death penalty for the Rosenbergs, the flimsy excuses for indicting Lattimore, the absurd indignities to which civil servants are subjected, the attorney general's use of the FBI files for partisan purposes, the Oppenheimer case, the possibly unconstitutional outlawing of the Communist party, and last, but far from least, the many squalid state and local measures against "subversives"—these events make a pattern. Some of them occurred before McCarthy's ascendancy, most of them afterwards, in none of them was he directly involved; but who can deny that he has contributed to them by aggravating preexisting repressive impulses, by encouraging his political enemies to try and beat him at his own game, by the fears that his mere presence on the national scene arouses?

Like the Nazis and Stalinists, McCarthy's stock-in-trade is a conspiracy theory of politics. Insofar as the Communists are an active conspiratorial group rather than a broad social category like the German Jews or people "of bourgeois origin" in Russia, they are at present numerically insignificant and the job of crushing them is too easily and too soon completed for them adequately to serve as totalitárian victim. Here, however, McCarthy's most authentically totalitarian traits reveal themselves: he constantly broadens his proscribed minority to include not only Communist party members but anyone opposing him who ever had any commerce with the party, real or imaginable. Weissberg, Beck and Godin, and other refugees from the Russian purge of the 1930s have reported that the first question asked by the GPU examiners and one which they relentlessly pursued throughout all questionings was "Who recruited you?" McCarthy too displays less interest in the witnesses appearing before his committee than in finding out who recommended them for government employment, who hired them, and who gave them security clearance, thereby expanding his proscribed minority to include ever-swelling numbers of potential victims. He has even placed "Communist thinkers" and all New Dealers stained by the "twenty years of treason" on the list.

As Hannah Arendt has pointed out in *The Origins of Totalitarianism,* organization is the *sine qua non* of totalitarian movements. It is the power of organization, both openly flaunted and working in the darkness, that lends reality to the "ideological fictions" of the movement. McCarthy's agents in the executive branch of the government, his "plants" among newspapermen, and his partisans in patriotic societies give the impression of constituting a diffuse conspiracy, if not a tightly controlled and centralized one. Its similarity to past Communist networks has been remarked on by many observers; totalitarian and semitotalitarian movements almost invariably imitate the organizational features of their enemies. McCarthy's apparatus functions secretly through an army of informers and openly, not by paramilitary formations marching in the streets, but by batteries of publicity. When leading national figures must debate McCarthy's wild charges as if they were a pressing national issue, they indeed become a pressing national issue. And when the government employs his flexible criteria of "loyalty" to evaluate its personnel, reality is conferred on McCarthy's claims, just as the Nazi storm troopers were able to equate "race" with personal destiny by beating up Jews in the street. What occurs here is the bureaucratization through enactment into law of the "ideological fictions" of McCarthyism, just as the racist fantasies of the Nazis were converted into impersonal juridical standards by Himmler. Even if McCarthy is soon discredited, his conception of the "Red menace" has been, so to speak, objectified and is able to outlive his personal political power.

It is necessary to emphasize once more that these similarities between the McCarthyites and the Nazis do not suffice to make the former a coherent fascist movement. They are similarities of "form" rather than of historical content. But they amount to an unmistakable injection of the totalitarian mentality into American political life. If McCarthy has simply galvanized the tendency to restrict civil liberties that emerges in all periods of actual or imminent war, he has nevertheless been successful enough to leave his own imprint upon it. If he should be repudiated by the professional politicians and his power at the polls revealed to be grossly exaggerated, the trend away from civil liberties will be to some degree arrested and the air will certainly be cleared. Yet his departure will not remove the pressures on civil liberties.

Too many intellectuals are addicted to apocalyptic modes of thinking: unless they can represent their enemy as a colossal force of evil threatening all liberal values, they become complacent and make little effort to combat more limited dangers. This applies equally to those liberals—often retaining illusions about Stalinism—who magnify McCarthy's power by picturing him as an American Hitler, and to the "hard" anti-Communists, concerned only with the admittedly greater worldwide menace of Soviet expansionism, who think that they have taken an adequate "stand" on McCarthy by showing that he is not a fascist, that he actually helps the Communists, and that his power is precarious. There was a time when a single case of injustice would evoke from the intellectual community a cry of protest that was free of ulterior ideological compulsions. Today one group of liberals responds to McCarthyism in escapist fashion by so exaggerating the urgency of combating it that all the more perplexing problems of modern politics are made to seem unimportant by comparison. Another group, aptly labeled "the petrified anti-Stalinists" by Philip Rahv, appears to feel that until blood is actually spilled in the streets McCarthy is no cause for concern. Yet whatever Mc-Carthy's political fate may be, resistance to the garrison state ideology and the defense of civil liberties will continue to be necessary. To build an effective dam one does not have to believe in the imminence of a deluge.

III McCARTHYISM: CONSERVATIVE INTERPRETATIONS

William F. Buckley, Jr., and L. Brent Bozell

THE QUESTION OF CONFORMITY

William Buckley, author of God and Man at Yale and Up from Liberalism, is editor of the National Review, a journal of conservative opinion. L. Brent Bozell is a contributor to the National Review. The book from which the following section is drawn is the most extensive literary defense of McCarthy. Much of the text centers on the controversy between Senator McCarthy and the Tydings Committee in 1950 over the alleged infiltration of the State Department by Communists, which McCarthy had charged.

McCarthyism, we are saying, has narrowed the limits within which political proselytizing can safely go forward in the American community. The assertion that there is a "reign of terror" directed at all who disagree with Senator McCarthy, we are saying further, is irresponsible nonsense. But something is abroad in the land, and we have no objection to its being called a "reign of terror" provided it is clear that a metaphor is being used, and that the victims are the Communists and their sympathizers. We may concede that America has come to insist on "conformity," if you will, *on the Communist issue.*

One of the problems that arises is that of stating precisely what the conformity, encouraged by McCarthyism, actually involves: *what sanctions* are being imposed upon *what people* to discourage *what sort* of activity. Defining the conformity is difficult, if for no other reason than that its shape and coloring vary sharply from one part of the country to another and from one field of activity to another. Another question entirely is whether we approve of the sanctions and of their being visited on the particular people they are being visited on. But there is a third question: What about the argument underlying the liberals' determined assault on McCarthyism—the argument that "conformity," *in any area whatever,* is undesirable? A number of serious writers on the subject profess to be disturbed not so much with the peculiar orientation of a "conformist" society, as with the fact that a conformity—*any* orthodoxy whatever—should exist at all. McCarthyism is bad, we are told, and must be bad, just

From William F. Buckley, Jr., and L. Brent Bozell, *McCarthy and His Enemies* (Chicago: Henry Regnery Company, 1954). Reprinted by permission of the publisher.

to the extent that it obstructs the free flow of commerce in the "marketplace of ideas."

The objection requires thorough consideration—not because it is profound, but because it elicits reflexive and emotion-charged support from so many people who, for excellent reasons, are concerned with protecting "freedom of the mind."

Opposition to conformity of *any* sort arises from a failure to understand the ways of society, a failure to recognize that *some* conformity, in varying degrees and in diverse fields, has characterized every society known to man; and for the reason that some conformity is just as indispensable as some heresy.

The word "conformity" is too often used to connote collective adherence by an insensate and irrational society to an unimaginative and erroneous doctrine. Thus the frequent references to the "threat of conformity," to "arid conformity," to "stultifying conformity," and so on. The word "conformity" is not necessarily misused when it is given that meaning. But it is also a useful word to describe the prevailing value preferences of *highly civilized societies;* and in that sense conformity may be a blessing rather than something to be avoided. In short, we rightly deplore the "conformity" obtained in Germany during the thirties—the orthodoxy which evokes so vividly the image of an authoritarian, secular, ethnocentric society, savage in its elimination of dissidents. But we may also speak of the "conformity" of English sentiment on, say, the subject of parliamentary government—and with some enthusiasm. In the one case, a nation was wedded to an evil social doctrine which it defended by imposing brutal punitive sanctions upon dissidents. England, however, is wedded to what we deem a highly commendable political process —and wedded to it by the voluntary acquiescence of all, or nearly all, of its citizens.

Our indictment of Nazi conformity is therefore based on two counts: (*a*) we don't like the values the Nazis encouraged, and (*b*) we don't like the fact that they violated persons who disagreed with them. Our approval of England's conformity with parliamentary rule is based on our approval of the institution of popular government, and also on our approval of the fact that Englishmen are not embarked on an active campaign against dissidents.

The conformity we are concerned with in this book—the one McCarthyism is promoting—resembles the English conformity on the first count: the vast majority of Americans are certainly in sympathy with those values communism threatens. It is equally clear—as regards the second count—that McCarthyism (understood as including all the legal, economic and social measures that are being used to discourage adherence to communism) has little in common with pogroms and concentration camps. But on this score the conformity encouraged by McCarthyism is not like contemporary English conformity either: for it *is* a calculated, purposeful national campaign levelled against Communist dissidents. Do we conclude, then—from this difference—that conformity, English-style, is desirable, while conformity, McCarthy style, is reprehensible?

It is easier to understand the conformity McCarthyism is urging, and the sanctions being used to promote that conformity, if we recognize that some coercive measures—i.e., restrictive sanctions of some sort—against dissidents are indispensable to the achievement of *any* conformity. *Coercion takes different forms.* It may be exercised through education, through social pressure, or through laws. But it must be exercised in one form or another if naturally diverse minds are to form a common tendency.

What liberals fail to understand is that even the orthodoxies they approve of have not come about through spontaneous consent. To act as though the Paraclete had, one bright morning, breathed into the hearts of Englishmen their allegiance to parliamentary rule is, among other things, to do a severe injustice to the thousands of men who devoted their lives to dislodging British absolutism. England had to fight for her form of government; and it was several hundred tumultuous years before popular rule emerged as the imperious and unchallenged orthodoxy that reigns today.

In short, we are apt to forget that conformity, in order to "be," must first "become." We cannot have our cake without first baking it. England's conformity with parliamentarism does not, today, depend on coercive measures to preserve its supremacy, because it is *mature,* because it is institutionalized to the point that it goes virtually unchallenged. McCarthyism, however, involves an orthodoxy still-in-the-making; and therefore, as with all imperfect conformities, some coercive sanctions are being exercised in its behalf.

The sanctions imposed on behalf of favored values have often been violent, as when the guillotine was used as an instrument for winning converts to French republicanism, or when civil war and the

Thirteenth Amendment were adopted as deterrents to slavery in this country, or when the Income Tax was written into our laws to encourage financial support of the government. Or, the sanctions may be relatively gentle: for example, the ubiquitous pressures which, for two decades now, have emanated from the classroom and from the bureaucrat's desk, from political podiums and from a preponderance of our literature, in behalf of the leviathan state.

The sanctions imposed by McCarthyism are of both kinds. The legal sanctions, the anti-Communist *laws,* are, in a sense, "harsh" measures. The Smith Act, for example, punishes with imprisonment anyone who conspires to advocate the overthrow of the government by force. The McCarran Act harasses members of fellow-travelling organizations. The Feinberg Law denies employment to teachers who are members of subversive organizations. Miscellaneous laws and executive orders deny government employment to persons regarded as loyalty or security risks.

The social sanctions of McCarthyism are of the other, relatively mild variety—as when individual schools refuse to hire Communist professors, or radio stations close their doors to Communist artists, or labor unions deny membership to Communist workers. They are ordinarily milder because, in the absence of a law on the subject, there may be other schools, radio stations, and unions that will give the Communists shelter.

To sum up, then, a drive for some conformity, and the turbulence often attendant on such a drive, are not unusual phenomena in our society or any other. And judging by past experience, if Americans, by the year 1999, learn to despise fellow-travelling with the same intensity and unanimity with which today they regard, say, slave-owning, it is predictable that the liberals of that day will not bewail America's anti-Communist orthodoxy.

But we must probe deeper into the alleged threat to freedom of the mind posed by McCarthyism. Although the measures by which McCarthyism encourages conformity are clearly the same measures by which societies *have* traditionally protected favored values, liberals are not obliged to *approve* of what societies have done in the past. They can repudiate *all* sanctions designed to influence opinion, past, present and future; and they seem to be doing this when they universalize about the evils of "thought control" each time the subject of McCarthyism is brought up.

It is perfectly true that the sanctions of McCarthyism (like those that have been used in the past on behalf of democracy, freedom for trade unions, and so on) *do* constitute "thought control" in the sense that they hack away, and are intended to hack away, at opposition to certain values. But to condemn these sanctions is to condemn the natural processes of society.

Freedom of the mind, we are told by the liberals, is an absolute value; and thought control, "since it impairs this freedom," an absolute evil. Few liberals are aware that the first of these statements does not necessarily justify the second. The only freedom that an individual may never sacrifice is, providentially, one that he will never be without: the freedom to act as a moral agent *at the choice level*—to select, as between whatever alternatives are left open to him, the one which most closely coincides with the "good." In religious terms, man's only absolute freedom is his freedom to earn salvation; and this freedom is irrevocable because man has a free will. The Russian serf, even within the area in which he is allowed by the state to act, can triumph over evil every bit as decisively as can the American freeman.

There remains, however, the alluring *political* argument that if democracy is to prosper, sanctions must not be used to delimit the number of ideas our minds consider, or to make one idea appear more attractive than another. Democracy, so the argument goes, thrives on the "free market in ideas," and to tamper with the market is, ultimately, to sabotage the machinery that makes possible enlightened self-government. In a democracy, therefore, every idea must be allowed to display its inherent attractiveness, so that it can be judged on its merits. All ideas must, so to speak, start out even in the race; and if an idea is to be rejected, this must be done by each individual for himself—free from coercion by his fellow men. McCarthyism embodies such coercion. Thus, *ipso facto* it is anti-democratic.

Unquestionably, the claims of the free market in ideas are very strong. Hard experience through centuries has taught us to exercise self-restraint in insisting upon our own notions of what decisions society should make. Societies, we have learned, fare better when they have a wide selection of ideas from which to choose, if only because their citizens are then better able to articulate, and therefore to realize, their wants. But when the liberals go on from here to formulate an inflexible doctrine which, in the name of freedom of the mind, would prohibit a society from exercising sanctions of *any* sort, and when they talk as if even the freest society could manage this feat, they are talking very dangerous nonsense.

Part of the liberals' difficulty is that when they think of sanctions against ideas, they think in drastic terms. They think in terms of denying employment to, or imprisoning the carriers of, "objectionable ideas." They ignore altogether the areas in which the process of "controlling" thought takes a less dramatic form. They do not consider, and hence do not weigh, the more subtle, but infinitely more important sanctions through which societies defend favored ideas.

Our schools, for example, have thoroughly indoctrinated the average American with the virtues of democracy. A sanction of the subtle variety has been exercised; and one that will unquestionably affect his political judgment in a thousand ways favorable to one favored concept—the perpetuation of democracy. Where, again for example, social disfavor attends Jew-baiting, a sanction (not the less effective because it is subtle) is being imposed against racial intolerance. Once again, does anyone contend that polygamy is getting a fair break in the market of ideas?

In short, every idea presented to our minds, as we grow up, is accompanied by sanctions of approval or disapproval which add to, or subtract from, that idea's naked appeal. And these sanctions are "thought control"—whether they urge political conformity with democracy by jailing Communist conspirators, or aesthetic conformity with classicism by disparaging, in the classroom, musical romanticism.

The practice of thought control is so ubiquitous and so commonplace as to make us wonder at the success of the liberals in frightening people with only one, the crudest, of its many manifestations. They turn the trick, it seems, by dramatizing the sanctions that are deliberately and purposefully imposed, while keeping silent about the haphazard process by which society subsidizes approved prejudices and preferences. And they disarm us by an impressive array of swear words which they apply only to the overt, dramatic type of sanction.

Not long ago, in the course of upholding (on the grounds of precedent) the constitutionality of Atlanta's banning of the movie *Lost Boundaries* (which dramatizes, among other things, the evils of Jim

Crow), a U.S. District Court launched into a ringing liberal lament, excoriating all such laws. The fate they deserve, the Court insisted, is "interment in the attic which contains the ghosts of those who, arrayed in the robe of Bigotry, armed with the spear of Intolerance, and mounted on the steed of Hatred, have through all the ages sought to patrol the highway of the mind."

The judge apparently disapproved the action taken by Atlantans to forbid the propagation of certain ideas on their screens. This, he suggested, was "thought control." Yet the question cannot be avoided: does the *withholding* of the ideas embodied in *Lost Boundaries* from audiences in Atlanta constitute "thought control" in some sense in which the *presentation* of those ideas to New York audiences does not? Was the Atlanta Board of Censors tampering with freedom of thought in some sense in which a dozen movie producers do not regularly do, month in month out, as they decide what pictures advocating what ideas shall be produced? Clearly, the *encouragement* of certain ideas on race relations can affect thought, just as the *discouragement* of these ideas can—as, for example, when they are suppressed. We may feel that it is a mistake to suppress such ideas; that Atlantans would profit from a sympathetic presentation of a Negro family's assimilation by white society. Yet this is merely a euphemistic way of saying that we would like to influence contrarily disposed minds in the direction of our own point of view—which is to plead guilty to the charge of thought control. We are certainly not less guilty than our fellow countrymen in Atlanta, who seek to incline minds the other way.

In short, it is characteristic of society that it uses sanctions in support of its own folkways and mores, and that in doing so it urges conformity. What we call the "institutions" of a society are nothing but the values that society has settled on over the years and now defends by sanctions. Most of us take fierce pride in our society's institutions—quite reasonably, since it is our institutions that make us what we are. But it is well to remember that in exhibiting this pride, we are applauding just so many manifestations of conformity which were brought about by the practice of "thought control" through many generations.

Not only is it *characteristic* of society to create institutions and to defend them with sanctions. Societies *must* do so—or else they cease to exist. The members of a society must share certain values if that society is to cohere; and cohere it must if it is to survive. In order to assert and perpetuate these values, it must do constant battle against competing values. A democratic society, for example, dare not take for granted that the premises of democracy will, unaided (i.e., solely in virtue of their ideological superiority), drive communism out of the market. If the contest were to be adjudicated by a divine tribunal, society could sit back with folded hands and watch the show. But it is not; and hence a concomitant of man's selecting freedom as against communism is his acting rationally in *behalf* of freedom and *against* communism. If the contest were to be adjudicated by a divine tribunal, a society could afford to be capricious and patronizing towards the enemy's ideas. It could even afford to act on liberal premises relating to "freedom of the mind" —by seeing to it, for example, that the *New York Daily Worker* circulated as many copies as the *New York Journal American.*

A hard and indelible fact of freedom is that a conformity of sorts is always dominant, as evidenced by such minutiae as that the *Journal American* and the *New York Post* are more heavily subscribed than the *Daily Worker.* And since a conformity of sorts will always be with us, the freeman's principal concern is that it shall be a conformity that honors the values he esteems rather than those he rejects.

This is not to say, of course, that society never makes mistakes in this area, and that the conformities selected by societies are, invariably, conformities with the eternal verities. Even free and enlightened men may use the power of sanctions in behalf of false and inferior values. But democracy is meaningless unless, having brought to bear on today's problems their intelligence, their insights, and their experience, freemen take vigorous action on behalf of the truth as they see it.

Thus liberal spokesmen, who are forever warning us against attempting to get an inside run for our favored values, show a fundamental misunderstanding of the free society.

The liberals are forever warning us about the dangers of coming down hard on those who oppose the basic values of our society. The Communist problem, for example, according to one of the liberals' favorite lines of argument, is not inherently different from that which, prior to the Revolutionary War, our forefathers posed to the English; and we have no more business assuming our own infallibility vis-à-vis the Communists than the English had in assuming theirs vis-à-vis the American Revolutionaries. "In 1940," writes Alan Barth, "the Alien Registration Act forbade all Americans to teach or advocate the duty or necessity of overthrowing by force or violence a government created by just such advocacy."

Two implications are clearly present in such a statement, namely, (a) that the revolution America is seeking to frustrate through the Smith Act and, one supposes, through McCarthyism in general, cannot be written off as morally reprehensible unless we are prepared to write off, in like manner, the Revolution to which we owe our existence as a nation; and (b) that the English ought not to have resisted our insurrectionary forefathers.

Both of these notions, we contend, are false, and the freeman must reject them as a matter of course: the one as contrary to his considered estimate of communism, the other as politically egocentric to the point of sheer naivete.

We believe on the strength of the evidence, that the American Revolution against George III was a revolution in the interests of freedom and of civilization. But it does not follow that the English should have recognized it as such, and should, accordingly, have given it their blessing. Still less does it follow that the Communist revolution is in the interests of freedom and of civilization, and that we should give it *our* blessing. For each free society must decide these questions by its own lights as they arise, and there is no place to which it can turn for the kind of guidance that will exclude the possibility of error. Certainly not to such doctrines as "the divine right of revolution."

The individual freeman may, of course, find himself in disagreement with his society's decision. If so, it is his duty to resist the majority, even if it be very large, to just the extent called for by the intensity of his disagreement. But let him not deny society's right to consolidate around the institutions it favors. Or at least let him not deny this right in the name of a free society.

The preaching of the liberals on the subject of conformity, as we have already suggested, does not conform with their practice. In the light of their own habits, their sense of outrage in the presence of McCarthyism becomes difficult to explain. For where movements are concerned that conform with liberalism, the liberals talk out of the other side of their mouths.

The drum-beating for a "bipartisan" foreign policy, for example, insistent and deafening as it was during the postwar years (and is even today), is a call for "conformity" in one aspect of public affairs. And who has beat that drum more assiduously than the liberals? Every time a diehard crosses the aisle and joins the bipartisan ranks there is jubilation in the liberal camp. That no such acclamation greets the regeneration of a Louis Budenz, a Whittaker Chambers, or an Elizabeth Bentley, is something for which the liberals have yet to offer a convincing explanation.

Where were the liberals when the weapons they now forbid us to use against the Communists were being used, fifteen years ago, against American fascists and against a number of Americans who were *not* fascists? And how do the liberals account for their past and present ruthlessness in assaulting all persons, groups, or even ideas, that are out of harmony with the liberal orthodoxy? That liberal weapons have been effectively wielded, many a businessman, many a so-called isolationist, and many a hard anti-Communist can prove by pointing to his scars.

What is more, the liberals have been signally successful in many of their drives for conformity. Not many years ago, for example, most Americans believed employers were entitled to recognize or not recognize labor unions as bargaining agents for workers as they themselves saw fit. But more and more Americans became convinced that the ends of social justice would be better served if workers enjoyed a stronger bargaining position. The liberals, however, were not content with a slow evolution of public sentiment. They were in a hurry. And no sooner did they win a Congress and a president of their persuasion, than they passed a law making collective bargaining *mandatory*. The nonconforming employer could thenceforward (a) close up shop or (b) go to jail for contempt. It was, to be sure, the employer's actions rather than his thought that the Wagner Act was intended to control. But it has also proved an extremely effective instrument of creeping thought control, since it has produced a gradual consolidation of public opinion around the ideas of its authors. If the collective bargaining clause of the act were repealed tomorrow, a few employers might conceivably turn the unions out. But an overwhelming majority would not. Sixteen years of collective bargaining, sanctioned by law and by society, have so deeply implanted this practice in our public morality that it has become, quite simply, an American "institution."

The liberals, in short, do want conformity—with liberalism. The overriding sin, in their attitude toward McCarthyism as a drive toward conformity, is their duplicity. The fulminations of those liberals who know what they are about are prompted not by a dread of conformity as such, but by the approaching conformity with values to which they do not subscribe.

To say that all societies encourage conformity leaves open the question of *how* they ought to encourage it. And there is a consensus that a society concerned with preserving individual freedom will not take away from dissidents one iota of freedom that does not *have* to be taken away in order to protect its institutions.

The traditional view among libertarians has always been that freedom tends to be maximized for both majorities and minorities, and thus for society in general, if social sanctions are preferred to legal ones. This view has normally been supported by two arguments: (a) that the *genus state* (which goes into action when legal sanctions are imposed) has natural aggressive tendencies that tend to feed upon each successive new grant of power; and (b) that social sanctions more accurately reflect the real "lay" of community sentiment.

The first of these arguments is grounded in long centuries of experience which have taught us that the state has attributes one of which is a tendency to usurp functions that can be equally well and, in most cases, better performed by the citizens acting individually or through voluntary and spontaneous associations. The end result of such usurpations is, of course, fatal to freedom. Thus wisdom instructs freemen not to whet the state's always enormous appetite for power by passing laws that add *unnecessarily* to the paraphernalia of the state.

The second argument rests upon what we have learned in the long pull of history about the plight of dissenting minorities, even in the freest societies. A legal sanction is, in theory, 100 percent effective: all the citizens are made to conform, even if only 51 percent of them entertain the views that prompted the legislation. Thus half the citizens of the state of New York, plus one, can through control of the legislature, pass a law that will prevent Communists from teaching in any state school—even though half of the community, minus one, believes such a law to be bad or at least inadvisable. Social sanctions, by contrast, are effective roughly in proportion to the number of persons who wish to exercise them: if only 51 percent of New Yorkers want Communist teachers kept out of the schools, and only social sanctions are used, then Communists will be kept out of, roughly 51 percent of the schools; the minority is left free to resist the pressure exerted by the majority.

In other words, minorities remain freer when majorities content themselves with the degree of conformity they can achieve without calling in the police. Freemen, other things being equal, will ardently desire to maximize the minority's freedom; and to the extent that they do they will advocate social evolution rather than legal revolution. The freeman who objects to nudism may inflict social indignities on the sun cultist, but he will not advocate legislation outlawing nudist colonies. The freeman will join in making life uncomfortable for Gerald L. K. Smith, but will not back a law forbidding Smith to publish his scurrilous literature.

It is interesting that the liberals have been far less concerned than libertarians about freedom for the minorities. They have a congenital fondness for passing laws, and a congenital distaste for waiting around while social sanctions engender conformity on this issue or that. The sure and swift machinery of the state fascinates them the way a *real* pistol fascinates youthful admirers of Hopalong Cassidy; their faith in it knows no bounds. Thus, for example, the proposed federal Fair Employment Practice Law is a sturdy rallying point for all liberals; while the libertarian prefers to encourage racial conciliation through education and social pressures.

The balanced libertarian does not, to be sure, hold that the majority members of a free society must *never* be "in a hurry," and that in no circumstances may they take the short cut conveniently provided by the statute-book. He well knows there are times when legal sanctions must be used, and he knows we live in such times today. He will advise the majority not to adopt *unnecessary* legal measures of a restrictive character; but not to hesitate to adopt the *necessary* ones, i.e., those that the exigencies of the situation clearly call for.

Mr. Justice Holmes laid down a famous test by which free societies can distinguish between the unnecessary and the necessary in this area. The "clear and present danger" doctrine is useful, and, probably, the best we have. The doctrine is, of course, incapable of furnishing wholly objective and unvarying standards, as Supreme Court experience with it has proved. But the central meaning of Holmes' test is clear and serviceable as applied to deeds as well as speech. It authorizes the use of legal sanctions against any activity that offers an imminent threat to the survival of existing institutions, or an imminent threat to the safety of persons or property. It forbids their use against all other deeds and utterances, and insists, indirectly, that a free society, when not in jeopardy, protect its values through the use of social pressure.

However we translate Holmes' test, most of us are agreed that activity on behalf of the enemy in time of war poses a clear and present danger.

We cannot avoid the fact that the United States is at war against international communism, and that McCarthyism is a program of action against those in our land who help the enemy. McCarthyism is (and, in our opinion, is likely to remain), nine parts social sanction to one part legal sanction. But that one part legal sanction is entirely legitimate. The resulting restrictions on a minority's freedom are certainly mild when compared with the drastic restrictions the majority imposes upon itself through such measures as military conscription. It is perhaps the crowning anomaly of present-day liberalism that it should, on the one hand, sanction the total tyranny of compulsory military service, and yet balk restricting the least freedom of our enemy's domestic allies.

Finally, the liberals insist, our society cannot, even during wartime, afford to cut itself off from *innovation.* Whatever the emergencies of today, the argument runs, we must think about tomorrow. We must make sure that our conformity shall not be so rigid as to barricade our minds against new ideas. The most terrifying nightmare of our intellectuals is that America may some day pass the hemlock to a Socrates, hang a Thomas More, or force a Galileo to recant. It can happen here, we are warned, if we give McCarthyism its rein.

This argument forgets that societies are, after all, educated as well as educable. It is one thing for society to give a hearing to new ideas, and quite another thing for it to feel impelled to put new ideas —simply because they are new or unorthodox—on a plane of equality with cherished ideas that have met the test of time. It is, for example, one thing to study Jean Paul Sartre and allow the free circulation of his books (which this country is doing) and quite another thing to give existentialist ideas the inside run in the curriculum of our university philosophy departments (which this country is not doing). It should after all be clear that a free market in ideas ceases to be free or a market if the latest huckster to arrive can claim his share of trade without regard to the quality or appeal of the commodity he is selling, and merely because he is a parvenu. The liberals, bewitched as they are with the value of innovation, tend to forget that a free market is one where the customers can, if they so wish, keep on trading with the same old butcher.

Moreover, the argument tends to equate "innovation" with progress. The innovator can regale society with a cornucopia of wealth and happiness; but he can also open a Pandora's box. A measure of healthy skepticism about new ideas is not a sign of obscurantism —nor, necessarily, an indication of stagnancy. Most of what we correctly call progress is a matter of the natural development and growth of old ideas. The statement that the heterodoxy of today is the orthodoxy of tomorrow, which we hear so often in this connection, is a piece of absurd oversimplification. *One* of today's heterodoxies may become tomorrow's orthodoxy; but if so, then, by definition, the remainder will not. And today's heterodoxies are always numerous in a way that the cliché fails to recognize. Witness in our country the brief flowering and unlamented demise of Know-Nothingism and Ku-Kluxism—both of them heterodoxies that did not, on the morrow, become orthodoxies. Nor is it true, as the argument suggests, that there is net social gain, or progress, necessarily and as a matter of course, every time a heterodoxy displaces an orthodoxy. Societies often progress backwards.

Even so, progress *does* occur, and no intelligent society should adhere to a conformity so rigid as to make the airing of alternatives dangerous or impossible. Our major differences with the liberals in this area have to do with whether McCarthyism tends in any such direction. And this brings us, at last, to the question: What is the actual extent of the conformity McCarthyism seeks to impose?

McCarthyism's Call to Conformity

McCarthyism, on the record, is not in any sense an attempt to prevent the airing of new ideas. It is directed not at *new* ideas but at Communist ideas, of which the last thing that can be said is that they are new or untried. The McCarthyites are doing their resourceful best to make our society inhospitable to Communists, fellow-travelers, and security risks in the government. To this end, they are conducting operations on two fronts: (1) they seek to vitalize existing legal sanctions, and (2) they seek to harden existing anti-Communist prejudices and channel them into effective social sanctions.

Valid laws and auxiliary Executive Orders prohibited Communists —or persons about whose loyalty or reliability there was a reasonable doubt—from holding government posts long before Senator McCarthy started talking; but they were frequently evaded, and sloppily administered. McCarthy and his allies have simply insisted that they be vigorously enforced. McCarthyism is primarily the maintenance of a steady flow of criticism (raillery, the liberals call it) calculated to pressure the president, cabinet members, high officials, and above all the political party in power, to get on with the elimination of security risks in government. In a sense, the major "victims" of McCarthy's drive for conformity have been those responsible for the so-called loyalty program, whom he has tried to inch into performing their clear legal duties.

On the second front, McCarthy has tied into fellow-travelers who have no tangible affiliation with the government. For example, he early aimed his fire at Harlow Shapley, Frederick Schuman, and Owen Lattimore. McCarthy exposed their party-lining and did what he could to build up social pressure against them. He has not, or at least not yet, succeeded in eliminating them from positions of power and influence in national academic life: all three continue to teach at important universities. But there is no doubting the fact that they are less influential than they were before. Their pronouncements on foreign policy are no longer cited as authoritative. Lattimore's future books about solutions in Asia are unlikely to become bestsellers.

The conformity attendant upon McCarthyism, then, adds up to something like this: (1) *persons who conspire to overthrow the government by force* are subject to legal sanctions (the Smith Act, for example), primarily that of imprisonment; (2) *persons in public service about whose loyalty or security there is a "reasonable doubt"* are subject to legal sanctions (the various security regulations), primarily that of exclusion from government employment; (3) *persons other than government employees about whom there exist reasonable grounds for believing they are "pro-Communist,"* are to some extent subject to legal sanctions (possibly the McCarran Act or the attorney general's list of subversive organizations), primarily that of having their activities officially labeled as "Communist" or "subversive" or (as with the Feinberg Law or the statutory loyalty oath requirements) that of being excluded from certain jobs; they are furthermore subject, increasingly, to social sanctions, primarily of the type that have been aimed at Lattimore and Schuman and Shapley.

These sanctions are not the same all over the country. In some localities, in sections of the Midwest for example, the sanctions hit people who might escape them elsewhere. In the rare instance, a single Communist-front affiliation may engender public hostility and bring down severe social sanctions on a man's head. In the academic arena of the East, by contrast, the level of enforced conformity is decidedly lower, and sometimes descends nearly to zero. Southern Baptist College X fires Jones when there are apparently no reasonable grounds for believing him to be a pro-Communist. But Harvard, Williams, and Johns Hopkins retain Shapley, Schuman and Lattimore on their faculties when reasonable grounds abound for believing them to be pro-Communist.

The claim is often made that McCarthyism has as its ultimate objective the exclusion of liberals from positions of power, prestige, and influence in the American community; and that the present campaign against Communists and fellow-travelers is merely the thin edge of the wedge. It is therefore curious that the one instance which lent a modicum of factual support to this fear received little or no attention from liberal publicists.

In October of 1952, Senator McCarthy delivered his widely heralded attack on Adlai Stevenson, which people generally expected would turn into an attempt to connect the Democratic candidate with communism. With millions of listeners glued to radio and TV, McCarthy reached, not for a red paint brush, but for a list of some of Stevenson's top advisors: Archibald MacLeish, Bernard De Voto,

Arthur Schlesinger, Jr. Was his point that these men were *Communists?* No, that was not McCarthy's point. His objection to these men was not that they were Communists, or even pro-Communists, but that they were liberals—atheistic, soft-headed, anti-anti-Communist, ADA liberals. And his major point turned out to be that this was sufficient reason for rejecting the candidate for whom they were serving as Edgar Bergens.

Whether the speech was a conscious effort to narrow the limits of tolerable opinion so as to exclude left-wing liberals, only McCarthy can say. The fact that he has not reiterated the point suggests that, if this *was* his intent, he was not very serious about it. It is far more likely that he intended to deliver a traditional political campaign speech highlighting the disqualifications of his party's opponents. But it may well be we have not heard the last of his idea. Some day, the patience of America may at last be exhausted, and we will strike out against liberals. Not because they are treacherous like Communists, but because, with James Burnham, we will conclude "that they are mistaken in their predictions, false in their analyses, wrong in their advice, and through the results of their actions injurious to the interests of the nation. That is reason enough to strive to free the conduct of the country's affairs from the influence of them and their works." But the real point, for our purposes, is that the mainstream of McCarthyism flows past the liberals as gently as the Afton; and that the MacLeishs, De Votos and Schlesingers have no grounds for arguing that any sustained effort is being made to read *them* out of the community.

It is still only *Communist* ideas that are beyond the pale. And the evidence is convincing that the function of Senator McCarthy and his colleagues is not that of defining or creating a new orthodoxy with which individuals are being called upon to conform. The American community affirmed anti-communism long before McCarthy started in. McCarthy's function has been to harden the *existing* conformity.

We are left with the final question: whether the conformity urged by McCarthyism is doing a service to America and, therefore, whether we should view it with approval. Certainly the vast majority of the American people have already given *their* answer to the question; for, after all, the approaching conformity is of their own making, and they must be presumed to approve what they are doing. Most Americans, the available evidence seems to say, favor anti-communism, and tight security in the civil service. But we are asking, of course, whether the majority is *right;* and therefore we must take account of the misgivings of the intelligentsia. What should be said of their resolute and impassioned opposition to McCarthyism?

Simply this. They are confused, they have misread history, and they fail to understand social processes. What is more, they do not feel the faith they so often and so ardently express in democracy. There is only one alternative to this explanation: that they are opposed to the decline of Communist influence at home. The determination of the American people to curb communism cannot be dismissed as a capricious, ignorant, or impetuous decision. There is, we contend, a great deal of difference between a society's harassing the exponents of an idea that has been thoroughly examined and found objectionable, and its harassing the exponents of an idea simply because it hurls a novel challenge at traditional notions. Our Schumans, Shapleys, and Lattimores have become unacceptable not because they are known to hold ideas and values at variance with those of the majority of Americans, but because they expound a *particular* set of ideas and values which Americans have explored and emphatically rejected, and because the propagation of these ideas fortifies an implacable foreign power bent on the destruction of American independence.

The ideas of the Schumans, Shapleys, and Lattimores are not, as we say, new ideas; they are exploded ideas. America has had access to the literature of communism for more than a generation. Everything from *Das Kapital* and *The Problems of Leninism* to monthlies, weeklies and dailies reflecting the least adjustment in the party line, has for years circulated freely in American classrooms, libraries, and living rooms. Communist missionaries have roamed the land to urge their ideas through the spoken word. In short, America could hardly have given communism a fairer or more exhaustive hearing without inviting over a dozen commissars to conduct an American Five Year Plan.

Having heard the case, America has rejected it. And because the case is championed by a mobilized, aggressive, titanic enemy state, America has gone further: she has turned to the offensive against communism. We are at war, and there are many strategies, many tactics, many weapons, many courses of action open to us. Our lines could be advanced by innumerable enterprises, some foolish, some proper—by assassinating Malenkov, by atom-bombing Soviet industrial plants, by subsidizing a Russian underground, by providing leadership and funds for prominent European and Asiatic anti-Communists, by imprisoning violators of the Smith Act, by purging the civil service, and by exposing and persecuting Communist apologists in whatever occupation they are engaged. One thing is certain: communism will not be defeated—any more than freedom was won —by postulating the virtues of democracy and of Christianity as evident truths and letting it go at that.

McCarthyism, then, is a weapon in the American arsenal. To the extent that McCarthyism, out of ignorance or impetuosity or malice, urges the imposition of sanctions upon persons who are *not* pro-Communist or security risks, we should certainly oppose it. When persons about whose loyalty or security reliability there is *no* reasonable doubt are flushed from government service for security reasons, those responsible should be criticized and held to an accounting both at the polls and before investigating committees. Whenever the anti-Communist conformity excludes well-meaning liberals, we should, in other words, go to their rescue. But as long as McCarthyism fixes its goal with its present precision, it is a movement around which men of good will and stern morality can close ranks.

Willmoore Kendall

McCARTHYISM: THE *PONS ASINORUM* OF AMERICAN CONSERVATISM

The late Willmoore Kendall, former member of the political science faculties at Yale University and the University of Dallas, is the author or translator of several works in political theory. He is the author of John Locke and the Doctrine of Majority Rule *and co-author of* Democracy and the American Party System.

My purpose in this chapter is neither to bury Joseph R. McCarthy, nor to praise him. As for burying him, that was done many years ago by more competent, and far more eager, hands than mine. As for praising him, that, like damning him, seems to me to have entered upon a phase in which everybody merely spins his wheels. The basic claims put forward on both sides—we should bless McCarthy's memory, we should rue the day he was born—no longer change; the claimants do not listen to, or even hear, one another, would not understand one another even if they did listen. They are likely, from now on, to persuade only themselves, and those who already agree with them. My purpose, I say, is neither to bury McCarthy nor to praise him but rather, starting out with one simple, noncontroversial statement about the McCarthy episode (perhaps the only noncontroversial statement that can be made about it), to raise and try to answer one simple question, which statement and which question I propose to put as follows: There were "McCarthyites," and there were "anti-McCarthyites," and they got mad at each other, very mad, and stayed mad at one another—if anything, got madder and madder at one another—through a period of several years. And the question arises: What exactly was everybody so mad about? What was the issue?

Or, to expand the statement a little, there was a fight, if not a war at least a long, sustained battle; heavy artillery was brought into play on both sides; men fought in that battle with the kind of bitterness and acrimony that human beings appear to reserve for those

From Willmoore Kendall, *The Conservative Affirmation* (Chicago: Henry Regnery Company, 1963). Reprinted by permission of the publisher.

occasions on which brother fights brother, cousin fights cousin, Damon—yes, it was often so, as I can testify from personal experience—fights Pythias. For a long while smoke hung thick over the field of battle, so that visibility was poor and there was great confusion on the part of the observing public, not merely as to how, at any given moment, the battle was going, but even as to what precisely the fighting was about—as to what exactly was getting decided, as to what actually the victor, once he emerged triumphant, would have won. Moreover, so thick was the smoke that the combatants themselves often became hazy in their minds, even differed among themselves, as to who was whose enemy and as to the sense in which this or that "enemy," if he was an enemy, was an enemy. At the time, therefore (and even for a long while afterwards), the question I raise here—What was everybody so mad about?—probably could not have been answered in a satisfactory manner. There had to be time first for the smoke to clear, and then for McCarthy to be buried, and, finally, for McCarthy to be praised and damned to such a point that no single laudatory or vituperative word that could be said about him remained still to be said.

By now, however—so at least I like to think—it should be otherwise; not only has the smoke lifted, but we have a whole generation among us who know of the battle only by hearsay; if we cannot answer the question now, we never shall be able to answer it. And it would, I submit, be sickening to have to conclude, as conclude we must if we cannot answer my question, that the fight was over nothing you can put your finger on; that the energies and heartaches that went into it were wasted energies and wasted heartaches; that, most horrible of all to contemplate, nobody won, nothing got decided, and it was all sound and fury, signifying nothing. My question, though simple, is also a grave question: either the McCarthyites and anti-McCarthyites got that mad at each other for some good and intelligible reason, or we all (for all of us of a certain age were, I suppose, one or the other, McCarthyites or anti-McCarthyites) made colossal fools of ourselves; and if we did we had best now face up to it, lest tomorrow we go make fools of ourselves again.

Now let us, for the moment, postpone my question and, fixing attention on the statement itself, pause to say several things about it that need to be said in order to place it in its proper context.

First, that this sort of "getting-mad" is not usual in American politics. Our politics, as Professor Clinton Rossiter has observed at length in a recent book, tend to be "low-key" politics, politics that precisely do not divide men on issues that are mad-making. And I have myself argued, in a book I wrote several years ago with a collaborator, that the *genius* of our political system lies in the sloughing-off of genuinely controversial issues—sloughing them off in order for them either to be handled outside the system itself (or better still, to be handled not at all, that is, suppressed or as some- times happens, repressed—into the deep recesses of our collective unconscious, where, providentially, we can forget all about them). The McCarthy phase, or episode, or set-to—call it what you like— was then something presumptively special in our political history, something that we must not expect to explain to ourselves with everyday concepts and everyday tools of analysis. It was no mere quarrel, for example, over allocation of the contents of the porkbarrel or whether a businessman from Kansas City is to be confirmed as ambassador to Ghana.

Secondly (that is, the second thing that needs to be said about how mad everybody got), we must not take for granted that the real issue ever, at the time, actually got put into words, ever actually thrust itself into the consciousness of the actors in the drama. To assume that the real issue was what got talked about—so we are assured by, variously, marriage counselors and trade-dispute arbi- trators, all of whom are in debt here to the greatest of female political scientists in America, Mary Follett—to assume such a thing, they say, is to show ignorance of the way quarrels among human beings generate and develop. John and Mary may *think* they are quarreling about whether to send Jo-Ann to Mount Holyoke or Chicago, and end up getting very mad at each other about it, and staying mad weeks on end. But not so, says the marriage counselor; the issue must be one that goes to the very depths of the marriage relation between John and Mary. What is really being fought about is Mary's feeling that John somehow does not treat her as an equal, or if not that then some far-reaching sexual maladjustment that neither John nor Mary would dream of articulating and may not even be aware of, or John and Mary's shared but inarticulate feeling that John has turned out to be a second-rater in his profession. The quarrel, according to Miss Follett and her followers, must go on and on about this basically irrelevant issue or that one, go on and on and get worse and worse, either until it is repressed or until the real issue is somehow brought out into the open and, with or without the help of an outsider, dealt with on its merits.

Thirdly—a similar but not quite the same point—the chances are that the real issue, once out in the open, will prove to be far more "important" and difficult than the issue over which the quarrelers think they have been quarreling; that, concretely, it will prove to involve the meaning and quality and above all the destiny of the relatedness of the quarrelers. He who delves into the depths of a quarrel, an honest-to-goodness, bitter, and sustained quarrel, must not expect to come up with peanuts, or any known equivalent of peanuts.

Two other small points of that kind and we shall have done with preliminaries:

1. The McCarthyites were mad at the anti-McCarthyites, and the anti-McCarthyites were mad at the McCarthyites, which, I am saying, is unusual in our low-key politics. But to that I must now add (not, as I am tempted to do, that the anti-McCarthyites were madder than the McCarthyites—angrier, more bitter, more ready to paste someone in the nose—because that would perhaps slosh over into the controversial) that what is most unusual, and a different matter altogether, is that the anti-McCarthyites got mad at all. For the anti-McCarthyites were the liberals; and the liberals, as I understand them, have some built-in reasons for not getting mad that the McCarthyites, the anti-liberals, do not have—built-in reasons connected, as I understand the matter, with the whole metaphysical and epistemological stance of contemporary American liberalism. That is to say, the liberals are usually the Tentative Ones of contemporary politics: they believe that everyone is entitled to his point of view, that in general one man's opinion is as good as another's, that, as I like to put it, all questions are open questions. Officially, therefore, they don't get mad—have, in point of fact, got really "fightin'" mad only twice within the memory of living man—once, of course, at Adolph Hitler, then a few years later and on their own principles equally unaccountably, at Joe McCarthy. Let us be quite clear about this. When *A* gets mad at *B* and sets out to defeat him cost what it may, *A*, whatever his metaphysics and whatever his epistemology, ends up saying, and saying in the most eloquent manner possible, which is by his actions: *B* is *wrong* about the issue over which we

have fallen out, and *I* am *right.* Now *A*'s metaphysical and epistemological commitments may or may not admit of his making any such
assertion; if *A* is a liberal, they certainly do not admit of it, because
the Master, John Stuart Mill, taught above all that one does not
assert one's "infallibility." In asserting it, *A* postpones until later
(perhaps, as in the two cases mentioned, until the Greek kalends)
a day of reckoning that, properly speaking, he has no right to side-
step (and along with it, the day on which he will get back to normal,
which is to say: not be mad at Stalin, not be mad at world communism, not be mad at Khrushchev—because who can say, after all,
who is right and who is wrong in politics?). Yet, I am saying, *A* the
liberal did get mad at Joe McCarthy, did set out to defeat him *coûte
que coûte,* did proclaim to the four winds that McCarthy was wrong
and he was right. And this, I suggest, forces upon us a slightly
revised but still more fascinating version of my original statement,
namely that everybody got mad, including the professional Tentative
Ones, the professional Don't-get-madders. At the same time, it lends
color to our suspicion that the issue actually at stake went very deep,
and never got itself stated in satisfactory terms. (As for the McCarthyites, they, unlike the liberals, have built-in reasons for getting
mad; they are the Non-tentative Ones of our politics, the Absolutists,
the people who couldn't care less if they get caught assuming their
own "infallibility." We have, therefore, less reason to be surprised at
their getting mad. They are on the point of getting mad, and for
good reason, all the time.)

2. We might profitably, though without making too big a thing of
it, remind ourselves of the other issues about which Americans,
despite their low-key politics, have had big quarrels in the past.
Mercifully, there have been very few of them; and conspicuously
absent from among them, mercifully again, have been the Constitution, the Bill of Rights, and, surprisingly perhaps, the Amendments
to the Constitution posterior to the Bill of Rights. Let us, by way of
background, tick them off: During the years 1776–79 there was the
issue of *Loyalism,* which resulted in our driving the Loyalists into
Canada. In the early years of the Republic there arose the issue of
the Alien and Sedition Acts—which resulted in the silencing, nay,
the persecution, of the alleged seditionists. During the years just
before and during the Civil War, there was the issue of slavery. All
three, I say, are cases where Americans got very mad at one another.

They stayed mad for a long time, and were determined not to compromise, or let the matter drop, but to *win*—either to repudiate or perpetuate the authority of the king in parliament, either to enforce or get rid of the Alien and Sedition Acts, either to abolish slavery or to save it as the South's "peculiar institution." And all three, as we can see in retrospect, involved an issue that bore, in the deepest and most direct manner possible to imagine, on the very destiny of the American people. All three involved, that is to say, a question that the American people must answer in order to know themselves as the kind of people they are, in order to achieve clarity as to their identity as a people, their mission in history, their responsibility under God—so, at least in those days, they would have put it—for the kind of political and social *order* they were to create and maintain in history. All three, let us note finally, are cases in which people kept on being mad until somebody won, and was understood by both sides to have won, and so made good its point about the destiny of America.

So much for preliminaries. I turn now to my question, and I propose to work my way toward an answer to it by taking up, then rejecting, in good Socratic manner, some "easy" answers that for one reason or another (as I hope to show) simply will not do. They are, as the reader will guess from my reference to Socratic method, the answers you will get if you go buttonholing people down in the market place, putting the question to them, and listening attentively to what they come up with. I got mine by bringing the question up one evening in the spring of 1962, at a "stag" dinner party made up of professors of political science at a well-known East Coast university. I shall, for convenience's sake, assign numbers to them, and devote a section of the present chapter to each.

Answer Number One

The issue was Joe McCarthy himself. McCarthy was rude, ruthless, fanatical. He lacked, as the good Mr. Welch put it, all "sense of decency." He was a master of demagogy, of, to quote the Federalist Papers, those "vicious arts, by which elections are too often carried." He reflected a mood of "hysteria" among the electorate, was himself hysterical, generated hysteria in others. He did not play politics according to the rules of the game as we understand them

here in America. His conduct, as a Senate majority finally got around
to putting it, was unbecoming a senator and a gentleman. He browbeat witnesses. He took advantage of his senatorial immunity in
order to blacken the reputations and assassinate the character of
innocent persons; like Fr. Coughlin, like Gerald L. K. Smith, like
Fritz Kuhn himself, he was a hater, a know-nothing, a man who knew
and spoke no language other than that of hatred. He represented,
in any case, a tendency that had to be nipped in the bud—lest it
develop into an American version of that which it most resembled,
namely, Nazism. He was, finally, a fraud; he never uncovered a single
Communist. All you had to do was *see* him, on television, in order
to realize that here was a man who must be struck down. What
more natural, then, than that he should divide the country into two
fanatically warring groups, namely, (*a*) those who like and go in for
that kind of thing—of whom there are always only too many, all
only too ready to respond with fury to any who resist them—and
(*b*) the rest of us, who cling to at least minimum standards of
civility?

That, I think, is a fair summary of the "case" against McCarthy as,
say, a *Washington Post* editorial might have put it in 1952, or as a
deeply convinced anti-McCarthyite (with, of course, a longer memory than most anti-McCarthyites have) would put it today.

Now, the McCarthyites among my readers would, no doubt, like
me to linger over the charges, one by one, and refute them—as, for
the most part anyhow, they have been refuted in The Book No
Liberal Reads, Buckley and Bozell. . . . I propose, however, to do
nothing of the kind, since one of the advantages of my simple
question—as compared to the questions on which discussion in
this area has turned in recent years—is this: it frees us from the
necessity of conducting the argument on that plane and enables us
to take what we may, I think, fairly call higher ground. It enables
us even to enter a demurrer—not, of course, to plead McCarthy
guilty as charged, but to plead that the facts, even if they were as
alleged, do not support the claim with which we are concerned,
namely, that we have before us an answer to my simple question.
The facts, as alleged, can at best illuminate only a small part of our
problem, and for the following easy-to-document reason: the Mc-
Carthyites and anti-McCarthyites were mad at each other, "fightin' "
mad at each other, before ever McCarthy appeared on the scene,

and long, long before he became chairman of the Committee on Government Operations. Which is to say, those who offer the answer before us are, quite simply, talking bad history and exaggerating out of all proportion the importance of McCarthy in the development of what I, at least, have no objection to calling McCarthyism. They are answering at most only a tiny part of our question, when what we want, what we must demand, is an answer to the whole question. McCarthy, like Achilles after the death of Patroclus, stepped into a battle that was already raging, one in which the lines were already drawn, one whose outcome he could and did still affect, but *not* one in which he could possibly become the issue being fought over. Never mind that the battle-waging armies ended up with new names —McCarthyites, anti-McCarthyites—because of his entry into the fray. Never mind, either, that the anti-McCarthyites do seem, as a matter of history, to have promptly got a lot madder at the McCarthyites than they had been before. Never mind, finally, that both armies increased considerably in size between the famous speech at Wheeling and the famous censure motion in the United States Senate. We are not asking why people got madder off at the end, or even why at some point the anger suddenly spread in ever-widening circles (as it did), but rather, What were people mad about to begin with? *What, for example, what were they mad about at the (earlier) time of the Hiss case?* What was the *real* issue? And the real issue was not, could not have been, McCarthy himself.

Answer Number Two

The issue was an issue between two conflicting views of world communism and the world Communist movement, between—I shall try here, as I did with Answer Number One, to put the thing from the side of the anti-McCarthyites, lest I be accused of stacking the cards in favor of the position with which, for good or ill, my own name is associated—those who are running scared in the presence of the so-called Communist threat, and those who are keeping their heads. Between those who would seek a false security by attempting to use against communism the Communists' own weapons, and those who are prepared to settle for that degree of security that is possible, who believe that security can be achieved with an arsenal limited to democracy's normal weapons, which are those of negotiation and persuasion. Between those who think that by striking out at the Communist danger in all directions at once we can somehow eliminate it, somehow conjure it out of existence, and those who have got it through their heads that communism, the Communist Empire on the world scene, the Communist minority at home, is something you have to learn to live with and ought to learn to live with because it is, after all, something that *we,* by our shortcomings, have brought upon ourselves. Between those who believe that the correct answer to communism is military force internationally and coercive thought-control domestically, and those who know that these are not answers at all, that the struggle against communism is a struggle over men's minds and hearts and souls, is in any case a battle that you win, if you win at all, by eliminating the poverty, the discrimination, the injustice, the inequality, that make communism attractive and give the Communists their strategic opportunities. Between those who see the Communist danger as imposing upon us a choice between liberty and security, and would unhesitatingly sacrifice the former to the latter, and those of us who know for one thing that communism is not that kind of danger, and know for another thing that the battle against communism is not worth winning if, in winning it, we must lose our freedom. Between those who attribute to the Communists supernatural, nay, miraculous powers of seduction, of deceit, of winning against even the most unfavorable odds, and those who know that the Communists are mere men like ourselves, no more able to infiltrate our councils, our institutions, our high places, than we are to infiltrate theirs. Between those who have somehow convinced themselves that the Communists never sleep, and those of us who know that Communists, like other people, need their eight hours in the sack. Between those who think the Communists actually believe in their so-called ideology: Marxism, the inevitability of Communist victory, etc., and those of us sufficiently knowledgeable to take that sort of thing with a grain of salt, to realize that what we are up against is not something new and different properly called the Communist Empire, but something old and familiar properly called Russian nationalism. Between those who think that a Communist dictatorship can keep on being Communist and keep on being a dictatorship for ever and ever, and those of us who know that dictatorships, including Communist dictatorships, mellow and go soft as they get old, and that revolutionaries, even the wildest of revolutionaries, grow conservative and cautious as they become habituated to power. Between those who think the Communists will stop at nothing, not even totally destructive universal war, in their bid for world empire, and those of us who know that the Communists, the Russian government and the Russian people alike, want, above all, peace. Between those so addled in their wits by communism that they think that even their next door neighbor may well be a Communist, and so see a Communist stripling behind every sapling, and those of us who remember, in the teeth of the Communist threat, that America is built upon trust among neighbors, that Americans do not sow the seeds of suspicion in each other's back yards. Between those who think the Communists really have found a way to repress, and hold in check, the forces that make for freedom in any society, and those of us who know that man's desire for freedom must in the end triumph over all obstacles. Between those who think the Communists mean it when they say they will "bury" us, and those of us who know that all that is just Communist "talk" and blustering. Between those who cling stubbornly to the notion that there are deep and irreconcilable differences between our so-called free society and the so-called slave society of the Soviet Union, and so take no cognizance of the political and economic and social change that goes forward within the Communist Empire, and those, better-informed, unencumbered by dogmatic preconceptions, who realize that with each passing day American society and Soviet society become "more alike"—become, each of them, a closer approximation to the universal society of the future, which will of course combine in beneficent union the better features of them both.

Answer Two is, clearly, a better answer than Answer One. It is, for one thing, better history. Through the period that we ought to have in mind when we speak of these matters, there have indeed been current among us two views of the nature and meaning of world communism, two views of which, as I like to think anyhow, the little rundown I have just given provides a not inaccurate summary; two views and, in general, two groups of "those who's," respectively committed to the one or the other; two groups, moreover, whose stand on a whole series of issues in public policy that arose through the period tended to reflect the one or the other of the two views. No harm is done, furthermore, by calling the one of the two views

the McCarthyite view and the other the anti-McCarthyite view—
provided, however, that we remember, here as before, that both
views had crystalized, and attracted numerous adherents, long before McCarthy appeared upon the scene; that the McCarthyite view
was not invented by McCarthy; that it had, indeed, through the years
in question, both more knowledgeable and more vigorous exponents
than McCarthy; that, in a word, *it had best be thought of as having
itself produced McCarthy rather than McCarthy it.* Insofar as it is
correct, then, Answer Two has the further advantage of being correct
for the whole period and not, like Number One, only for the years
immediately following the Wheeling speech.

One easily sees, moreover, why those who entertained the Mc-
Carthyite view tended to get mad at those who entertained the
anti-McCarthyite view. At least one of the two views, possibly perhaps both of them but at least one of them, must be wrong, intel-
lectually incorrect, which is to say they cannot both be correct.
Each of the two views, pretty clearly moreover, is pregnant with
implications about policy, both foreign policy and internal security
policy, that flatly contradict the implications of the other, so that any
time a policy decision has to be made in either of those two areas
the two groups are likely, other things being equal, to array themselves on opposite sides. Nor is that all. Since each view, from the
standpoint of the other, would commit the nation to policies certain
to turn out to be suicidal, we readily understand how and why the
two groups did get mad at each other early in the period, and got
madder and madder at each other as the period progressed. For
each, in the eyes of the other, was guilty of an error of judgment
so great as to seem unforgivable.

Indeed, Answer Two makes so much sense that we are tempted
to adopt it out of hand as the correct answer to our question, and
let it go at that. Our question is answered, and we can all settle
back in our chairs and forget about it.

I suggest, nevertheless, that we take (but hold until we are sure
we can do better) a rain-check on Answer Two as well as on Number One—not because Answer Two isn't correct as far as it goes
(which I have conceded it is), but because, to me at least, it seems
inadequate psychologically, and because its assumptions about the
articulateness of American political struggles are somewhat more
flattering than we deserve. Concretely, I find that Answer Two ex-

plains to me why some people got mad, but not why so many people got mad, or why anybody—to go back to my original form of words —got all *that* mad. The issue that Answer Two insists upon is (a) for the most part an issue about foreign policy, and I do not believe that Americans in general were at any time during that period that interested in foreign policy, and (b) an intellectual issue, where the ultimate crime the alleged criminals are being accused of is merely stupidity, and I do not believe we had yet reached the day when intellectual issues, issues ultimately capable of being talked out or, failing that, capable of being resolved by sound scholarship, arouse in us the kind of passions that were displayed in the clash between McCarthyism and anti-McCarthyism. Millions of the persons who rallied around McCarthy, I should guess, and hundreds of thousands (for I do not believe there were millions) of the persons who rallied against him, entertained no view whatever on the nature of communism, and, in any case, were not about to be moving in the direction of civil war against those who entertained a view different from their own. In other words, our correct and inclusive answer, if and when we find it, will tap a dimension that Answer Two conspicuously avoids, namely—for they were not a slip on my part, those words "civil war"—the civil war dimension, the dimension, if you like, of mutual accusations of heresy. And having said that, I can venture the following thesis: The ultimate crime of which McCarthyites and anti-McCarthyites were accusing one another was, make no mistake about it, that of heresy; the passions generated were, make again no mistake about it, passions appropriate not to an intellectual debate but to a heresy-hunt, and we shall not understand them, ever, unless we bear that in mind.

To which let me add, before passing on to Answer Number Three: if Answer Two were correct, people would evidently be madder today than they were in 1953, which in point of fact, as I have intimated above, they certainly are not. For the differences among us as to the nature and meaning of communism are no less deep, no less unresolved, than in 1952; nor, I feel safe in saying further, have the stakes, which I repeat involve the very survival of the United States, got any lower. The correct answer to our question, then, must be able to explain why the clash between McCarthyites and anti-McCarthyites seems not only not to have become sharper, but to be less sharp today than it did nine years ago; and Answer Two cannot explain that for us. The correct explanation, in short, must explain not only the storm, but also the apparent ensuing calm.

Answer Number Three

The clash between McCarthy and his enemies was merely another chapter in the history of the separation and balancing of power within the American political system. What was at issue was neither differing views of communism as such (the clash might equally well have occurred over some other topic), nor, to go back to Answer One, McCarthy himself as such (although, say the proponents of this view, McCarthy had personal qualities that made the dispute angrier than it would otherwise have been, perhaps even innate tendencies of character that disposed him to play the role of hysteria-monger), since the forces operating through McCarthy might equally have expressed themselves through some other leader. The issue was, rather, that of legislative encroachment on the constitutional powers of the executive. For one thing McCarthy pressed the prerogatives of congressional investigating committees to hitherto unheard-of lengths—as witness, for example, his apparent belief that those prerogatives extended even within the sacred precincts of the nation's universities. For another, even if we were to grant that Congress was acting within its constitutional powers when it put the Internal Security Program on the statute books (even if we were, *per impossible,* to grant that the program did not violate the freedom of speech clause of the First Amendment), still enforcement of the relevant laws was the proper business of the president and his subordinates in the excutive branch of government—with, of course, appeals where appeals might be required to the courts of law. McCarthy's attempts to intervene in the dispatch of individual cases, his explicit claim that the Committee on Government Operations was entitled to watch over and criticize the detail of internal security administration, therefore represented congressional self-aggrandizement in its most blatant and dangerous form. Nor is that all. McCarthy undermined discipline in the executive branch by openly inviting civil servants with tales to bear to break the chain of command and come directly to him; he would right all wrongs, punish all iniquities. Nor is even that all. The day came when foreign service officers were obliged to falsify their reports lest McCarthy haul them before his committee and, with his usual techniques of insinuation and innuendo, his usual willingness to assume a man guilty until proven innocent, crucify them for their alleged pro-Communist bias. Nay, still more. The day came when the foreign services could no longer attract able recruits because no young man in his senses would expose himself to the risks McCarthy had injected into the career of the foreign service officer; considerations alike of decency and of self-interest sent men of talent into other careers. Even McCarthy's "working capital," for that matter, the scraps of so-called information that he "held in his hand" and that enabled him to move in on his victims, came to him through violations of security regulations; his very possession of them was legislative encroachment. McCarthy, in short McCarthy every time he opened his mouth, upset the separation of powers equilibrium that is central and sacred in the American political tradition. He upset it, moreover (if we abstract from his having been a senator not a member of the House of Representatives), in precisely the manner contemplated by the founders of the Republic, namely, through the workings of a demogogically-led popular movement, adverse to natural rights and to the public interest, which sweeps through the country, establishes itself in Congress, finds itself unable to accomplish its objectives because of the defensive weapons the Constitution entrusts to the two other co-equal and coordinate branches of government—and must, willy-nilly, seek to concentrate all power in its own hands. The McCarthy movement did just that, and, naturally enough, all in America who love constitutional government, that is, limited government, saw in him a threat to all that they most value in the American political tradition, responded to him with righteous anger, struck back at him as best they could. Nor, on the anti-McCarthy side at least, is any other answer needed to the question, "Why did people get so mad?"

Here, moreover, as with Answer Two though not with Answer One, the supposed issue is neat and symmetrical, that is, joined in almost identical terms from the other side: The Internal Security Program, or Loyalty Program as it was called in its early days, went onto the statute books by virtue of the exercise by Congress of powers clearly vested in it by the Constitution. The executive branch of government, the Department of State in particular, refused from the first moment to recognize the necessity for such legislation. It called its constitutionality into question, showed a complete lack of sympathy both with its underlying principles and its objectives, openly defied it, did everything it could to frustrate the committees —the Internal Security Committee in the Senate, the Committee on Un-American Activities in the House—Congress charged with responsibility for studying and reporting upon the Communist threat. The executive withheld information from them (on the mostly spurious grounds of so-called classification), lied to them *ad libitum,* refused, even in the clearest cases, to act upon information provided by them—or, for that matter, upon information provided by their great ally within the executive branch itself, the FBI. The executive kept in positions of high authority and honored men who obviously could not meet the loyalty-security standards set by the Congress. It moved—through the Truman Loyalty Order of 1947, which arbitrarily shifted the administrative standard in loyalty cases so as to give to the individual not the government the benefit of doubt—to emasculate the program, starved the security offices in the great government departments, and mobilized against the program not only the formidable opinion-making resources of its bureaucracy but also those of the newspapers and the radio and television networks. Subsequently, after McCarthy's appearance on the scene as a subcommittee chairman, it denied Congress' crystal-clear right to inquire whether its statutes were being faithfully executed. If there was encroachment, then it was clearly a matter of the executive's encroaching upon Congress. Congress, off at the end, had no alternative but to raise up a McCarthy, and insist upon its right to exercise the investigative powers needed in order to prevent the executive from becoming, quite simply, a law unto itself. Nor could any man capable of grasping the clear language of the Constitution hesitate as to where, in the interests of constitutional government and of the American political system as traditionally understood, to throw his support. If McCarthy had not existed it would have been necessary, for the sake of constitutional equilibrium, to invent him; and, naturally enough, the people, jealous always of the powers of that branch of government which, because closest to them in point both of time and of distance, they regard as peculiarly theirs, rallied around him. As for abuse of investigative powers, the Supreme Court is always there to set metes and bounds for congressional committees, and the records contain *no* Supreme Court decision that rules adversely to the McCarthy Subcommittee.

The issue, I repeat, is neat and symmetrical, but as regards an answer to our question we are back, I think, to where we were with Answer Two. Some people no doubt got mad about legislative encroachment in the area of internal security, and some no doubt about executive defiance of the will of Congress. Both groups, no doubt, got madder still because of the continuing dispute over the nature and meaning of the world Communist movement; but also no one ever heard of anybody with a soft view of communism getting worried, in those days, about *executive* encroachment, or of anybody with a tough view of communism getting worried about *legislative* encroachment. Once again, therefore, the suspicion arises that we are flattering ourselves; that is, vastly exaggerating, this time, our capacity as a people to work ourselves up into a fury over an issue so legalistic and intellectual as separation of powers. The admittedly hard-to-read slogan emblazoned upon the banners of the McCarthyites, whatever it proclaimed, could not have proclaimed the principle: "All legislative powers herein granted shall be vested in a Congress of the United States. . . ." Answer Three is better than Answer Two in that it edges us over toward the kind of issue that could breed charges of heresy not stupidity. But we do not, I think, yet have hold of the right heresies.

Tests for a Correct Answer

I have now taken up one at a time, and examined, the three answers to our simple question that, as I put it to begin with, one is likely to encounter in the market place of contemporary American political discussion. I have in each case found the answer either unconvincing or, insofar as convincing, inadequate; that is, incapable of explaining the *whole* of the phenomenon that has engaged our curiosity. I should, however, be very sorry for the reader to conclude that we have wasted our time; that is, made no progress whatever with our task. For we have, I like to think, insofar as we have reasoned together correctly, begun to apprehend certain tests that a correct answer to our question must be able to meet, namely:

First, it must point to an issue deep enough to possess what, for lack of a better term, we may call *genuine civil-war potential,* an issue capable, therefore, of being mentioned in the same breath with the slavery issue, the Loyalism issue during the American Revolution, and the issue (about which, let me say, we know all too little) posed, very early in our history as a nation, by the Alien and Sedition Acts.

Second, it must be an issue that large numbers of people are capable of grasping with hooks that are not precisely those of the intellect—an issue capable, I am tempted to say, of being grasped intuitively, of being felt as well as thought. "As well as," mind you, not "rather than," for I do not wish to imply that it must be an issue not susceptible of being put into words, or an issue that wholly eludes rational discussion.

Thirdly, it must be an issue that, somewhere along the line, calls for an act, though not I should think necessarily a conscious act, of *moral choice* on the part of the man who "takes sides" on it. That is why I have stressed that one of its characteristics is that of not lending itself to resolution merely by sound scholarship, or to being just plain "talked out"—to a point where all may agree because all objections, on one side or the other, have been met and answered. That notion we may now refine a little by adding that it must be an issue that we would expect to be "talkable-outable," if I may put it so, only among men who move in their talk from common or at least reconcilable moral premises.

Fourthly, the issue must meet certain historical tests or requirements. We must be able to see why, as a matter of history, it might well have begun to make itself felt (again, I stress "felt," for it will not necessarily have been clearly articulated), why people began to get mad about it at such and such a period rather than earlier.

Fifthly, it must be an issue about which we can explain, not too unsatisfactorily, why it has seemed less sharp through the years since McCarthy's death than it did through the years preceding McCarthy's death.

Now, I believe, as the reader will have guessed, that I know what the issue is, and I am going to try, in the next and concluding section of the present chapter, to get it into words and "justify" it over against the tests I have just enumerated.

The Correct Answer

Let us go right to the heart of the matter. By the late 1930s, that is, by the end of the second decade after the Communist Revolution, every free nation in the world, whether it realized it or not, faced the following question: Are we or are we not going to permit the emergence, within our midst, of totalitarian movements? Every free nation, in other words, was by that time already confronted with evidence that efforts would in due course be made to call such movements into being, that such efforts would be strongly supported from the home bases of the existing totalitarian movements, and that those efforts could, to some extent at least, be encouraged or discouraged by the action of its own government. Most free nations, to be sure, chose to ignore that evidence, and did not pose to themselves the question I have named, not even in some more cautious form such as "Are we at least going to try to prevent the emergence here of the totalitarian movements we see flourishing in other countries?" Not so, however, the United States. By the mid-1940s it had on its statute books an impressive array of legislation—the great names here, of course, are the Hatch Act, the Smith Act, and the so-called McCarran Rider—which (a) reflected a very considerable awareness that the problem of encouraging or discouraging totalitarian movements existed, and called for some kind of answer, and (b) announced in effect: We—whatever other free nations may do or not do—are going to put certain major obstacles in the way of such movements; we at least are not going to facilitate their emergence; we at least are going to take some perfectly obvious immediate steps that should make clear alike to the self-appointed leaders of such minorities, to the world in general, and to ourselves, where we stand on the matter; and we at least regard the emergence and growth of such minorities as on the face of it undesirable. Let us proceed at once, then, to exclude representatives of such minorities from the service of our governments, national, state, and local; and let us proceed also to clip the wings of such minorities by forbidding them, on pain of imprisonment, to advocate the overthrow of the government of the United States. Opinions might differ, let us be fair and concede it at once, as to the moment the question narrowed in legislators' minds from one concerning totalitarian movements in general to one concerning a Communist minority in particular. Opinions might differ, too, as to the moment at which the Communist movement burgeoned, in legislators' minds, from the status of a logical possibility to that of a clear and present danger. Opinions might differ, finally, as to the moment at which the American liberals decided that the question as to the future of totalitarian movements in the United States came under the general constitutional rubric of so-called freedom-of-speech questions, and therefore under the rubric of actions permitted or prohibited to the Congress of the United States by the First Amendment to the Constitution. But all three of these developments did, in due course, take place; and we must, in order to approach the correct answer to my question, get them clearly in mind—first of all as background for the following (in my opinion) crucial points.

First, the motive that underlay the original internal security legislation was certainly *not* that of impairing or limiting the Communists' freedom of speech. The Communist being struck at was for the most part the Communist who precisely did not exercise his constitutional right (if any) to freedom of speech in order to advocate communism, but rather the man who, having transferred his allegiance from the United States to world communism, set out to systematically conceal the fact from his fellow-citizens. The "freedom" at stake in the early legislation, then, assuming there was one worthy the name, was not freedom of speech, which the First Amendment does forbid the Congress to impair, but rather, if a "freedom" we must have, freedom of thought—the freedom to entertain such and such opinions in the United States without being subjected to such and such disabilities and such and such disagreeable consequences. Freedom of *thought,* I say, about which the Constitution of the United States says nothing at all. (Never mind that the liberals say that when the Constitution says freedom of speech it means, must mean, freedom of thought. We have only their word for it.)

Second, the authors and supporters of the original legislation do not appear to have had, in passing the legislation, any freedom of speech "inhibitions," or for that matter any notion that the legislation they were putting on the statute books involved anything especially novel in the way of principle.

Thirdly, it was, nevertheless, not long before one began to hear, from liberal quarters of course, rumblings about freedom of speech, about the patent unconstitutionality of all such legislation, about, finally, the incompatibility of all such legislation with traditional American concepts of—of all things—freedom. The United States could not take preventive action against the emergence of a Communist movement because, precisely, of its commitment to liberty!

Fourthly, after a certain moment in this train of events, everything, as I see it, conspired to conceal the issue actually, really and truly being fought over; everything but, as I have already intimated, two things: (a) communism did at some moment acquire, in the eyes of Americans generally, the status of a "clear and present danger." And (b) the liberals, at some moment, did pull in their horns, did change their public stance on anti-Communist legislation. Up to that moment (or those moments) what debate there was turned on the question, " Is the United States entitled to impose disabilities upon an emergent 'political' movement deemed undesirable even if it is not a clear and present danger?" or, variously,

> Is there anything in the Constitution or in the American political tradition that prevents American government or American society from announcing: We intend to proscribe such and such "political" opinions; to that end we intend to persecute those opinions, that is, to place the price of holding them—not expressing them, but holding them—so high that people will be forced to avoid them or, if they have already adopted them, to abandon them?

Up to that moment (or those moments) what debate there was was a matter of the legislators answering that question in the affirmative and the liberals answering it in the negative. While after that moment (or those moments) the debate shifted to the very different question: "Is the United States entitled to strike at a body of opinion which constitutes a clear and present danger?", which question, because of the aforementioned shift on the part of the liberals, almost everyone, the legislative majority and the liberals alike, was suddenly answering in the affirmative. The original issue, in other words, simply disappeared, and, we may safely add, has hardly been heard of since.

Let me, so as to guard against any possible misunderstanding, say that over again in a slightly different way. First we get what amounts to the proscription of the Communist movement in America on the grounds merely that such a movement is undesirable in the

United States, and that the proscription of an undesirable movement is clearly within the power of Congress—clearly, and without any complications about impairment of "freedom of speech" or "clear and present danger." The liberals oppose the proscription, on the grounds that Congress has no power to proscribe—unless, just possibly, in the presence of a clear and present danger. A debate gets under way that, had the terms not changed, would have had to be decided one way or the other, yet could not have been decided one way or the other without (as I shall argue more concretely in a moment) what each party to the debate regarded as the very gravest implications as to the nature of our constitutional system. But the terms did change, because of two developments which, though more or less simultaneous, we must keep rigorously separated in our minds. First, communism became, in the eyes of people generally, the kind of clear and present danger in the presence of which even the liberals might concede Congress' power to act. Second, the liberals, pretty certainly on straight strategic grounds, suddenly decided that they not only might but would give their blessing to the proscription of the Communist movement as, or insofar as it was, a clear and present danger. The original issue, therefore, promptly disappears, since all that remains to be talked about is whether, or the extent to which, communism *is* a clear and present danger. The first development, in the absence of the second, would presumably have resulted only in redoubled effort on behalf of a course of action already decided upon before it occurred (just as more fire-fighting equipment is called in when what has seemed a routine fire suddenly threatens to become a conflagration). The second development, in the absence of the first (in the absence, that is, of a decision that the fire was not a routine fire), would merely have signalized overwhelming liberal defeat on the original issue—which would, accordingly, have been decided in favor of the legislators. But the second development in the context of the first could only have the effect of spiriting the original issue away. Which is what it did.

Now my thesis is that the issue that really divided the McCarthyites and the anti-McCarthyites was, precisely, that original issue; that once we see that to be true, everything falls into place; and that, to anticipate a little, the disappearance of that original issue was, any way you look at it, a major national misfortune. And it remains for me only (a) to note that the original issue is merely an alternative statement of the issue that political philosophers debate under the heading "the open society," (*b*) to show that things do, once we recognize that as the issue at stake between the McCarthyites and the anti-McCarthyites, fall neatly into place, and (*c*) to make clear why I regard its eclipse as a "major national misfortune."

Let me put it this way: All political societies, all peoples, but especially I like to think our political society, this *"people of the United States,"* is founded upon what political philosophers call a consensus; that is, a hard core of shared beliefs. Those beliefs that the people share are what defines its character as a political society, what embodies its meaning as a political society, what, above all perhaps, expresses its understanding of itself as a political society, of its role and responsibility in history, of its very destiny. I say that is true especially of our political society because in our case the coming into existence as a people, a certain kind of people with a certain conception of its meaning and responsibility, takes place right out in the open for all to see, takes place unshrouded by the mists of remote history or the hazes of possibly inaccurate legend. "We," cries the people of the United States at the very moment of its birth (and we should be grateful to John Courtney Murray for having recently reminded us of the fact), "We," cries the American people at that moment, "hold these *truths.*" That is, "we" believe there is such a thing as Truth, believe that the particular truths of which Truth is made up are discoverable by man's reason and thus by our reason, recognize *these* truths as those to which our reason and that of our forebears have led us, and agree with one another to *hold* these truths—that is, to cherish them as ours, to hand them down in their integrity to our descendants, to defend them against being crushed out of existence by enemies from without or corrupted out of all recognition by the acids of skepticism and disbelief working from within.

Now, such a consensus, conceived of as a body of truths actually held by the people whose consensus it is, is incomprehensible *save as we understand it* (in Murray's phrase) *to exclude ideas and opinions contrary to itself.* Discussion there is and must be, freedom of thought and freedom of expression there are and must be, but within limits set by the basic consensus; freedom of thought and freedom of expression there are and must be, but not anarchy of thought or anarchy of expression. In such a society by no means are *all* questions open questions; some questions involve matters so basic to the consensus that the society would, in declaring them open, abolish itself, commit suicide, terminate its existence as the kind of society it has hitherto understood itself to be. And it follows from that, as August follows July, that in such a society the doctrine according to which all questions are open questions, including, for example, the question as to the merits of communism, is itself one of the excluded beliefs—one of the beliefs that are excluded because they involve, on the face of them, denial of the consensus that defines the society and sets its tone and character. And, having said that, we can get down to cases. What the McCarthyites distrusted and disliked and got mad about in the anti-McCarthyites was the at first explicit then tacit contention: we in America can't do anything about the Communists because America is a society in which all questions are open questions, a society dedicated to the proposition that *no* truth in particular is true, a society, in Justice Jackson's phrase, in which no one can speak properly of an orthodoxy—over against which any belief, however immoral, however extravagant, can be declared heretical and thus proscribed. And what the anti-McCarthyites distrusted and disliked and got mad about in the McCarthyites was the at first explicit and then tacit contention: America is not the kind of society you describe; the First Amendment does not have that meaning; America is a society whose essence is still to be found in the phrase "We hold these truths"; it *can* therefore proscribe certain doctrines and beliefs, and in the presence of the doctrines and beliefs of the Communists it cannot hesitate; it must proscribe them, and preferably long before they have had an opportunity to become a clear and present danger. Moreover, the McCarthyites knew, instinctively if not on the level of conscious articulation, that the anti-McCarthyites had good reason (long after they had dropped their principled opposition to the internal security program) for continuing their opposition to it in the courts of law, for continuing to provide the most expensive of expensive legal talent for its so-called victims, and this quite regardless of whether or not they were so situated as to constitute a clear and present danger—had good reason because in their hearts they believed that no measures ought to be taken against the Communists at all. And the anti-McCarthyites knew that the McCarthyites, for all their willing talk of clear and present danger, had good reason for carrying the persecution of the Communists further, at every opportunity, than the clear and present danger doctrine called for; they believed in persecuting the Communists not because they were dangerous but because, from the standpoint of the consensus, their doctrines were wrong and immoral. Each group understood the other perfectly, and each was quite right in venting upon the other the fury reserved for heretics because each was, in the eyes of the other, *heretical.*

It is I repeat unfortunate for us all that the issue, once joined, did not stay joined, and that the question became so confused that each of the two groups emerged from the McCarthy period under the impression that it had won—the McCarthyites because they got the persecution of the Communists that their understanding of the American consensus demanded, and the anti-McCarthyites because the persecution went forward with the incantations appropriate to the clear and present danger doctrine. Why unfortunate? Because until that issue is decided we no more understand ourselves as a nation than a schizophrenic understands himself as a person—so that, again in Murray's words, the American giant is likely to go lumbering about the world in ignorance even of who and what he is. And because—dare I say it?—next time around, people are going to get a whole lot madder.

IV McCARTHYISM: POPULIST INTERPRETATIONS

Historical Critiques

Leslie Fiedler

McCARTHY AS POPULIST

Leslie Fiedler, a professor of English at State University of New York at Buffalo and contributor to many journals of literary and social criticism, is the author of Love and Death in the American Novel, The Second Stone, *and* Waiting for the End.

Even if we attribute to McCarthyism a whole atmosphere of suspicion of which it is a symptom rather than a cause, it can be said that its effects (I do not mean the firing of proven Communists, in which many anti-McCarthyites would concur, but the intimidation of all unorthodoxy and especially of the outspoken critics of intimidation) have been small in proportion to the anxiety they have created. I should suppose that the excessive fear of the "intellectuals," in so far as it is more than a tic of anxiety, is based on the suspicion that McCarthy represents not merely himself, his own ambition and chicanery, but a substantial popular hostility, immune to argument and logical proof, to their own *raison d'être*. Certainly, it was disconcerting to discover not many months back that the majority of the American people were favorably disposed toward McCarthy, despite the fact that the larger part of their semiofficial spokesmen were bitterly opposed to him. In a certain sense, McCarthyism not only fluorishes in but *is* this hostility between the community and its intelligence. An occasional intellectual apologist, whether an embittered "premature anti-Communist" like James Burnham or a black young radical like Buckley, makes little difference. The price of supporting McCarthy is self-abnegation, and there is no reward.

The forces that McCarthy really represents (I mean his mass support, not the Texas millionaires of whom so much is made; anyone who persists in politics in America, whether he be right or left or

center, McCarthy or the Communists or FDR, can get himself a
millionaire or two) find their expression in the resolutely anti-intellectual small-town weeklies and in the professionally reactionary
press, which continue to say in his name precisely what they have
been saying now for thirty-five years. To realize this is to understand that McCarthyism is, generally speaking, an extension of the
ambiguous American impulse toward "direct democracy" with its
distrust of authority, institutions, and expert knowledge; and, more
precisely, it is the form that populist conviction takes when forced
to define itself against a competing "European" radicalism. Mc-
Carthy is a new voice for these forces though scarcely a different
one, with his automobile salesman's pitch, his proffering of inaccuracy and the inability to stay on a point as evidence that he talks
the customer's language. The astonishing thing about McCarthy is
his closeness to a standard kind of midwestern political figure,
usually harmless and often comical. What defies analysis is the aura
of fear which surrounds him.

Certainly, the facts of McCarthy's early life add scarcely anything
to a comprehension of the phenomenon for which he stands. There
is so little in his career sinister or even calculated, and so much
clearly banal and accidental, that one who dislikes him finds himself tempted to overinterpret unfavorable data in a way embarrass-
ingly reminiscent of McCarthy himself. There is a quality in the man
that makes McCarthys of us all, unless we are content to accept a
paradox for our conclusion. He is not (though it would be com-
fortingly simple to believe so) any of the things we ordinarily mean
by the word "fascist"; and comparisons with Huey Long are beside
the point. McCarthy is not, to begin with, a spellbinder in the Hit-
lerian sense, but almost antirhetorical in his effect, confidential and
bumbling, an expert harrier of witnesses but a mover of masses only
in a queer, negative way. Certain crowds seem to find his very lack
of glibness an assurance that he is their voice—and quite inexpli-
cably they roar; but an even mildly sophisticated audience finds it
easy to laugh him down. He is not a racist, and, indeed, in the early
days of his career was opposed by the old-school, anti-Semitic native
Fascists. Though more recently he has been hailed and even supported by known anti-Semites, he has himself never been recorded
as playing on the racist fantasies common enough among his own
constituency; and his association with certain clearly identifiable

Jews like Cohn and Schine works in quite another direction. Indeed, when the latter two were on their famous quick European investigation tour, one sensed in certain of the adverse comments on them (the comparisons to Gallagher and Shean, for instance) the faintest and most polite undercurrent of anti-Semitism working in the anti-McCarthy direction. Moreover, one of the bitterest McCarthy onslaughts against the Voice of America was for cutting down its Hebrew broadcasts at a point when it might have been possible to make capital of the anti-Semitic tone of the Slansky trial in Czechoslovakia. Because it baffles a convenient stereotype if McCarthy is not a racist, the charge continues to be made, and American Jews as a group were in the middle of 1953 the only section of the population to oppose McCarthy by a large majority; but the verdict is at least: unproven.

Certainly, he has left behind the backwoods doctrine which identifies the Elders of Zion with the International Bankers, and the Bankers with the Bolsheviks; for McCarthy, communism is no diabolic expression of an outcast race, but quite simply the foreign policy of the Soviet Union. It would be ridiculous to claim for McCarthy (as he occasionally does for himself when visiting easy scorn on some innocent Army intelligence officer who cannot distinguish between Marxism and Marxism-Leninism) any real theoretical understanding of communism; he keeps a stock of experts on hand for such matters, satisfactorily repentant ex-Communists and an occasional amateur like G. David Schine, who once prepared a brochure on the subject for circulation in his father's hotels. McCarthy seems, however, to have been twice victimized by Communist *agents provocateurs,* once in the almost prehistoric days of the congressional debate on the Malmédy massacre, when he was completely duped by a German Communist called Rudolf Aschenauer, who apparently supplied McCarthy with manufactured evidence that American interrogators extorted confessions from German storm troopers by torture; and once when he was taken in by a young American Negro, Charles Davis, who offered faked evidence to prove that John Carter Vincent was in contact with Soviet agents. When McCarthy refused to recognize Davis, after the latter had been deported from Switzerland, Davis filed a suit for libel, confessing in the course of the proceedings that he had been a member of the Communist party. The combination of naiveté with an eagerness to accept any evidence against an enemy as true has made McCarthy the victim of almost as many frauds as he has himself perpetrated.

But it needs no sophistication to understand communism in 1954; history has defined for anyone with a sense of political fact what Marxism-Leninism has become—namely, the rationalization and defense of that which Russia or its agents do for the sake of expansion or self-defense. In the light of this, it is a little disingenuous to complain, as some critics have done, that McCarthy never defines in his books and speeches his key term, "communism." In the formal and academic sense, he certainly does not; but it is hard to deny that the term has been defined for him, as for all of us, with distressing clarity.

The story of McCarthy's life is at first glance disconcertingly the rags-to-riches idyl of campaign literature: the son of a poor Wisconsin farmer, he worked hard from childhood on, taking from his father a small section of land that, single-handed at the age of sixteen, he made into a paying poultry farm. Indeed, he seemed on the very verge of prosperity when he broke down from overwork; and, when he recovered, his ambitions had changed. He began the slow movement toward the big city which he has followed ever since, transferring first to the little town of Manawa, Wisconsin, where he became not merely the successful manager of a grocery store but the town's darling. Deciding that he needed an education to fulfill the hopes he had aroused in his fellow-townsmen, Joe finished an entire high-school course in the single year before he reached twenty-one, alternating extraordinary feats of memorization with equally fervent bouts of physical activity; and went on to Marquette University, where he soon switched from engineering to law, though he was a shy and awkward speaker in public.

In college, McCarthy became a boxer of considerable ability, learned painfully to debate, was elected president of his class, and was graduated without particular academic distinction. After two years of law practice, he entered a political campaign for the first time, being defeated for Shawano County attorney on the Democratic ticket, and decided, though he had glowed earlier with a hatred for Hoover in particular and the Republicans in general, that his future lay in their party. In 1939, at the age of thirty, he was elected judge of Wisconsin District 10, winning an utterly unforeseen victory. All his early political activity was characterized by an incredible willingness to take pains, a complete contempt for expert predictions, and a fantastically unflagging energy.

As a judge, he proceeded immediately to wipe out in a matter of months an apparently permanent backlog of 250 cases and never dropped behind in his calendar again, though keeping up meant holding court in session past midnight on many occasions. When the war came, he took a leave of absence from his judicial post to enlist in the Marine Corps, where he served as an air intelligence officer behind the front lines, volunteering from time to time to accompany bombing flights as an unofficial tailgunner. Before the war was over, he left the Marine Corps to enter national politics, making a first vain bid to get the Wisconsin senatorial nomination away from Alexander Wiley in 1944. He was finally elected to the Senate in 1946, after taking, in a victory that characteristically astonished everyone but himself, the Republican nomination from an overconfident Bob LaFollette, who had scarcely troubled to campaign.

Superficially the record is a cliché, embodying only too patly the Pluck and Luck of the legend; but one must accept as real the unquestioning will to victory (across his tent in Guadalcanal McCarthy hung a banner reading: "McCarthy for U.S. Senate," though he was willing to pass it off as a joke) and the compulsive drive toward hard work, which led McCarthy after his election to slip off anonymously and work in the wheat fields. He is an American instance, and must be understood in terms of our myths and compulsions rather than in adapted European terms.

It has often been alleged that McCarthy lacks principles; and certainly he is immune to most of the traditionally noble ones, desiring to succeed chiefly for success' sake and loving the feel of over-extended strength as an end in itself. To punish and be punished, to yield voluptuously to the fury of struggle—these *are* his principles, the fundamental values to which he is devoted. "I don't claim to be any smarter than the next fellow," he told a reporter after his election to the Senate, "but I do claim to work harder." One has the sense that he is reciting a part rather than making a statement. Though, as his name indicates, McCarthy's background is Irish and Catholic, he has none of the amiable fecklessness one associates with his stock; he is the puritan we all tend to become, with the puritan's conviction that the desire to win is the guarantee of being chosen, the gift of energy a sign of salvation. He has apparently

FIGURE 3. Senator Joseph McCarthy. (*Brown Brothers*)

never doubted this, though he was for a while uncertain of what end
he had been chosen for, aside from the important one of being Joe
McCarthy. But his discovery of the Communist issue settled his
doubts quickly, giving to his undefined conviction of a mission a
sanction at once religious and political. His notorious shopping
around for a cause up until 1950 must, in the light of this, be considered something far more complicated than simple opportunism.

A closer look at the record reveals the shoddy underpinnings of
the American legend—but this also is typical. From the start, Mc-

Carthy's career has been marked by broken promises and betrayals of confidence (his very first office was obtained behind the back and at the expense of his law partner, who had similar ambitions); and by a series of "deals," petty or large (beginning with the trivial episode of the high-school teacher wooed into making possible his record secondary-school career). His appearance of simple virtue goes to pieces under the most superficial scrutiny; though he has been able all along to establish legal innocence of various charges against him, he has emerged always morally indicted. In his early campaign for the judgeship, he apparently overspent the statutory allowance and in campaign literature consistently misrepresented his opponent's age; and even in his famous clearing up of the docket he turns out to have shown more haste than discretion. He connived in a series of astonishingly quick divorces for friends, personal and political, though it meant bypassing the divorce-counsel system of which Wisconsin likes to boast; and he attained special notoriety for not only acquitting the Quaker Dairy of unfair price practices on the odd grounds that the law involved would go out of date in six months, but also destroying a vital part of the court record. He seems also to have contravened the clear intent of a Wisconsin law forbidding judges to run for public office while maintaining tenure on the bench; he could not be convicted because he was running for federal rather than state office.

McCarthy's whole subsequent career has followed the same pattern: from the production of a pamphlet on housing for which he was paid $10,000 by Lustron, a private manufacturer of prefabricated housing, much interested in the legislation before McCarthy's housing committee; through his tangled relations with sugar consumers that earned him the nickname of the "Pepsi-Cola Kid"; to his long history of alleged misrepresentation and barely legal accommodation in preparing his income-tax reports.

It would be foolish to portray McCarthy as extraordinarily corrupt in these respects. He is a hopelessly ordinary politician in all things: his manipulation of his finances, his willingness to "arrange" matters behind the scenes, his barely legal maneuverings to escape uncomfortable restrictions. This is the standard procedure of the standard elective official, and is standardly revealed from time to time in standard investigations; but between such orgies of exposure

and righteousness the ordinary American voter not merely condones
but applauds evidence of such minor duplicity in his representatives
as a sign of political acumen.

McCarthy has been shown up, too, in another favorite practice of
the politician: the refurbishing of his own record and the blackening
of his opponent's by the discreet manipulation of truth. McCarthy's
election as judge at the age of thirty is not considered striking
enough: it must be made twenty-eight; his enlistment as a first lieutenant in the Marine Corps must be revised for public consumption
into enlistment as a private who then worked his way up through the
ranks. A job as an intelligence officer must become an assignment
as tail-gunner; a leg smashed up during horseplay aboard ship must
be turned into a combat wound, recognized with the Purple Heart—
and finally metamorphosed into "ten pounds of shrapnel" carried
with an exaggerated limp. It is possible that McCarthy does not even
consider such conventional accommodation of facts to be lying: he
seems especially proud of his own truthfulness, and whenever he
and some opponent come into absolute conflict over a question of
fact, he typically cries out for a lie-detector test with all the air of a
much-abused citizen turning to science to redeem him.

He practices in addition the college debater's device (I can dimly
remember my own debate coach recommending it to me with a
wink) of waving about irrelevant papers as he makes some especially undocumented statement. This is a clue, I think, to his whole
attitude, the "plain man's" conviction that figures are useful only
for bolstering after the fact an intuitive judgment or insight. Despite
his extensive research staff, and his recent willingness to do a little
homework on his charges, McCarthy seems still incapable of believing that it *really* matters whether there are 200, 205, 81, or 57
Communists in a certain branch of the government. He appears
clearly convinced that those of his opponents who concern themselves with such discrepancies are stupidly or insidiously trying to
divert attention from what truly matters: are there *any* Communists
in the department concerned?

It is tempting to identify McCarthy's lying with the Big Lie of Hitler;
but it seems more closely related to the multiple little lies of our
daily political forum, to a fact of our national life too often ignored by
those looking for analogies instead of roots. McCarthyism is, in part,
the price we pay for conniving at or ignoring the alderman's deal

with the contractor, the mayor's boast that he was always labor's friend. Yet McCarthy's distortion of the truth is not merely a particular development of the cheap politician's hyperbole; it is also the courtroom lawyer's unchallenged device for "making a case" rather than establishing a fact. The politically naive citizen called for jury duty in any town in the United States begins by being horrified at what seems to him at first a contempt for the truth, but is revealed later as the lawyer's assumption that *there is no truth*: that guilt and innocence are matters, not of moral judgment or even of established fact, but of a decision arrived at inside a devious technical code of procedure. But the naive are never horrified enough.

I do not place McCarthy in this context to justify him, but rather to condemn the system of which he is a pathological symptom. Anyone unwilling to believe how *like* most other lawyers McCarthy is should volunteer to serve on a jury; or, short of that, should read the reports of other congressional investigations, preferably of those with whose ends one is in general sympathy—of war profiteers, say, or of organizers of antilabor violence. It would suffice, perhaps, to read through the report of the Tydings subcommittee which condemned McCarthy to see how clearly such investigations distinguish between looking into facts and proving a case. To change the rules of *all* congressional investigating committees so that at least the safeguards of the courtroom will be provided for what has become a judicial procedure, to insist on the right of confrontation, representation by counsel, etc.—all this will help; but it will not solve the underlying problem I have tried to define. In certain ways, it would seem more desirable to make the proceedings of congressional investigation *less formal,* less like trial procedure, leaving to the courts the business of establishing technical innocence or guilt, and reserving for the legislative branch, as our national conscience, the task of seeking the truth of morality and feeling. One can imagine no person less equipped for such a task than the run-of-the-mill lawyer trained in the cynical school of the community courtroom.

But there remains in McCarthy's handling of the truth a more sophisticated and "modern" use of the lie than the politician's or the lawyer's. It is a concept of "symbolic" truth-telling, which has, of course, always existed, but which has entered into public life with especial vigor in recent years. It is tempting to call it a "totalitarian" concept, for it has been much exploited by Communists and Fascists;

but it is, alas, a favorite device of hard-pressed liberals and conservatives; once the process is begun on either side, the other seems forced to respond in kind. A McCarthyite will say, for instance, "There are hundreds, thousands of Communist espionage agents in the State Department," meaning merely that the influence of Communist ideas, at one remove or another, has helped determine State Department policy for the worse. To this the liberal will answer, "There is not a single Communist in the State Department and there has never been one," meaning simply that, "in so far as men and notions influenced by Communists have played a role in the State Department, they have been "idealist" in inspiration, and therefore have done more good than harm.

Or, on a more specific level, a McCarthyite will howl, "Lattimore is the top espionage agent in the United States," which translated means that Lattimore's ideas coincide remarkably with those of the Communists; to which the liberal answers, "He is entirely innocent, a good man," or decoded, "Well, whatever his ideas, they were ones that some quite close friends of mine agreed with once, etc." The Communists themselves have a "scientific" way of saying all this, making the charge, for instance, that the Jewish Social Democrats were "objectively" on the side of Hitler.

McCarthy, of course, is not capable of distinctions between objective and subjective allegiance, any more than he can distinguish between ends and means; but his intellectual and proto-intellectual supporters are quite willing to sustain him on these grounds both publicly and to themselves. There is no doubt in my own mind that Robert Taft, for instance, supported McCarthy (despite waverings and reservations) because he himself had long been convinced that "objectively" socialists were no different from Communists, and leftish New Dealers no different from either; so that calling any supporter of the "welfare state" a Communist might be rude and impolitic but was not actually wrong. Still, Taft was always a little *uncomfortable* about it all, as the handful of more intellectual fellow-travelers of McCarthyism continue to be uncomfortable.

The simple-minded McCarthyite, however, has no trouble at all; he is not disturbed about the problem of whether a lie can be objectively true, because a political lie does not seem to him to be morally reprehensible. McCarthy's position depends not at all upon fair play or respect for conscience, whereas the moral *raison d'être* of his opponents is their scrupulousness; and it is for this reason that these opponents, once betrayed into playing his game of symbolic truth-telling, are at a disadvantage. They find themselves in a terrible dilemma in this regard; granted the discrepancy between their values and that of the vast public, even the non-McCarthyites, they can hardly ever be quite candid without seeming to confess a guilt they do not feel; and, granted their morality, they cannot trifle with the truth without feeling a guilt they do not confess. . . .

Just as McCarthy is incapable not only of believing that those who disagree with him may be right, but even of granting that they may be wrong through misjudgment or normal stupidity; and as he is convinced that behind the opposition to him there is a conspiracy or plot; so his opponents fall into a similar belief. The plot discovered is the finding of evil where we have always known it to be: in the *other*. But the final joke and horror of the situation is that there *are* in our days conspiracies which baffle common sense. Even the most fantastic accusations of McCarthy are lent a certain plausibility by the revelations of the Hiss case, in which it scarcely matters whether you opt for the Communist-espionage-ring theory of Hiss's guilt, or the equally fantastic forgery-by-typewriter theory of his innocence. What an absurd world we live in where only half the audience, or less, laughs aloud when McCarthy charges that James Wechsler himself wrote the Communist editorials attacking him.

But the Red-baiter and the liberal do not really charge each other with equal conviction. The liberal is uncertain even when, closing his eyes in desperation (but all the time, he *knows*), he repeats ritually: "Lattimore is pure; Hiss was framed; the Rosenbergs are a mirage; there never was a Klaus Fuchs; Harry Dexter White was maligned. . . ." And as a final charm: *"No harm has been done, no harm has been done, no harm has been done!"* The McCarthyites, however, answer with more certainty (their eyes have always been closed and they do not even suspect it) and equal ritual insistence: "Yalta and China, Hiss and Marzani and Harry Dexter White; treason and the coddling of treason; *guilty, guilty, guilty!*"

It is no use protesting that McCarthy himself has revealed no dangerous hidden Communists; that the Marzanis, the Hisses, and the Rosenbergs of whom he boasts were turned up by other agencies, before the opening of McCarthy's much-advertised campaign. In so far as Joe McCarthy is an individual, he has proved little beyond the foolishness and uncertainty of many who have appeared before him; even his single prize, Lattimore, is no "espionage agent." But in so far as McCarthy is the personification of a long-inarticulate movement, of the sullen self-consciousness of a sizable minority, he *begins* with a victory that he cannot fritter away, no matter how many errors he makes or how many downright lies he tells.

The emergence of McCarthy out of the wreckage of the La Follette Progressive movement in Wisconsin is a clue to what he represents. He inherits the bitterest and most provincial aspects of a populism to which smooth talking has always meant the Big City, and the Big City has meant the Enemy. Traditionally that enemy has been identified with "Wall Street," but from the mid-1920s there has been a tendency to give an equal status to the nonnative rebels who claim also to oppose the bankers. Indeed, Robert La Follete, Jr., had gone so far in the latter direction that in 1946 the Communists, through the Wisconsin CIO council, supported McCarthy against him. It was not until 1950, however, that McCarthy discovered a symbolic butt in the State Department "Red," the "Park Avenue Pinko," capable of welding together the fractured Populist image of the Enemy. In light of this, it is just as important that McCarthy's initial attack was directed against the State Department under Acheson (and against Harvard behind him) as that it was directed against the Communists. Acheson is the projection of all the hostilities of the midwestern mind at bay: his waxed mustache, his mincing accent, his personal loyalty to a traitor who also belonged to the Harvard Club; one is never quite sure that he was not invented by a pro-McCarthy cartoonist.

With something like genius, McCarthy touched up the villain he had half-found, half-composed, adding the connotations of wealth and effete culture to treachery, and topping all off with the suggestion of homosexuality. McCarthy's constant sneering references to "State Department perverts" are not explained by his official contention such unfortunates are subject to blackmail, but represent his sure sense of the only other unforgivable sin besides being a Communist. The definition of the Enemy is complete—opposite in all respects to the American Ideal, simple, straightforward, ungrammatical, loyal, and one-hundred-percent male. Such an Enemy need not be *proven* guilty; he is guilty by definition.

It is interesting by way of comparison to see how much less sure

McCarthy is before even a scoundrel who shares his own "American" prejudices. Certainly, no traduced liberal has ever faced him down as he was faced down by Isador Ginsberg, a war profiteer and former leader of a veterans' organization, who appeared before McCarthy when he was on the housing committee. "I want to say, sir," the grey-marketeer cried out in the midst of the questioning, "Ginsberg is as proud as McCarthy. I don't believe you can possibly pass legislation to prevent me, and honest men like me, from making a fair profit. Only in Russia can that be done!" And McCarthy, an "honest man" like Ginsberg, after all, and no friend of Russia, had to confess he was right: that only the enemies of profit and the defenders of communism were outside the pale.

But the Enemy for McCarthy is not only a dandy, a queer, an intellectual, and a Communist; he is (or was, at least, in the beginning) a Democrat or a Democrat's friend. The struggle between the liberal intellectual and the old-line Red-baiter has been absurdly confused with the contest for votes between the Democratic and Republican parties. This seems, in part, clearly accidental. McCarthy himself was, for a while at least, a Democrat (his chief counsel Roy Cohn still proudly declares himself one); and at the start his charges were taken up largely as ammunition to be used against the ins, who happened to be Democrats, by the outs, who happened to be Republicans. It was possible at first to believe that there was no anti-Communist conviction at all behind McCarthy's campaign against the State Department, but merely a desire to slander his opponents and advance the fortunes of his own party; but one senses in him the happy coincidence of conviction and strategy. Blessed is the man who can at the same time gather in votes and vent the fear and hostility that the encroachments of Soviet imperialism have stirred in most American hearts! . . .

It was a strange and embarrassing opportunity for the Republicans, who found themselves on the popular side of an issue for the first time since 1932. In America anti-communism has never been an exclusively bourgeois attitude; indeed, the only sizable group ever to challenge it was completely bourgeois. It has always been strongest among farmers, unorganized workers, and the lowest level of the middle class; and, once McCarthy had brought into the open a problem which opposed to the People the Intellectuals rather than "the Economic Royalists," a new kind of Republican was needed to assume leadership, the kind of Republican represented on varying levels of respectability by Nixon and McCarthy. This Senator Taft, for instance, appears to have sensed; perhaps he knew all along that though he was called "Mr. Republican" he could not make the populist appeal. Certainly, in this light his otherwise inexplicable support of McCarthy, his willingness to tout him in speeches dedicated to "political morality," makes a kind of sense.

The votes which clinched McCarthy's first senatorial victory came not only from the wealthier Catholic farmers of Wisconsin but from the working-class districts of Kenosha and Racine and Milwaukee ordinarily considered safe for the Democrats. If there is a blackness in McCarthy, it is not the reactionary blackness of the oil interests or of the Catholic Church, but of something in the American people which grows impatient with law and order, with understanding and polite talk, when it feels it has been betrayed. The ordinary American who has for years thundered in his Legion post against Reds cannot understand why, at a time when we are being baffled by Reds on three continents and are actually committing troops to battle against them, there should be a single Communist or defender of the Communists in a position of trust. He is only enraged when one speaks to him of safeguards and due process; of the difficulties of adjusting from a period in which the Communists were not only a legal party but our allies; of the actual equivocal status of Communists under the law. The Army, caught up in the toils of its own involved legality, finds itself forced to promote a Communist dentist before it can discharge him; and those who always have equally distrusted red tape and Reds scream in anguish through McCarthy, who is their mouthpiece.

The spirit that speaks is fundamentally a lynch spirit, the cry of those convinced that recognized evil cannot be touched by the law: "Let's get them before it's too late. Let's do it now!" But the lynchings have been only verbal so far, moral lynchings, which compared even to the reprisals against radicals that followed the First World War appear relatively calm and sane. The fight against McCarthy must be carried on, but those who wage it must be aware that they are fighting a whole section of our people unable to understand a situation in which moral condemnation of a group has far outstripped the community's legal procedures for dealing with them. It is therefore hard to undercut McCarthy, especially because most of those who attack him have always been considered by his supporters to be their natural enemies; and because, more and more, the picture is established in the minds of his adherents of Joe the Giant-Killer—a limited but dedicated man, fallen among fast-talkers and slickers.

C. Vann Woodward
THE POPULIST HERITAGE AND THE INTELLECTUAL

C. Vann Woodward, formerly a member of the history faculty at Johns Hopkins University, is a professor of history at Yale University and the author of Origins of the New South, 1877–1913, Reunion and Reaction, and The Burden of Southern History.

During the long era of the New Deal one had little difficulty living in comparative congeniality with the Populist heritage. The two periods had much in common, and it was easy to exaggerate their similarities and natural to seek antecedents and analogies in the earlier era. Because of the common setting of severe depression and economic dislocation, Populism seemed even closer to the New Deal than did Progressivism, which had a setting of prosperity. Common to both Populists and New Dealers was an antagonism to the values of the dominant leaders of the business community bordering on alienation. They shared a sense of urgency and an edge of desperation about the demand for reform. And in both, so far as the South and West were concerned, agricultural problems were the most desperate, and agrarian reforms occupied the center of attention. It seemed entirely fitting that Hugo Black of Alabama and Harry Truman of Missouri—politicians whose political style and heritage were strongly Populistic—should lead New Deal reform battles. From many points of view the New Deal was neo-Populism.

The neo-Populism of the present bred a Populistic view of the past.

C. Vann Woodward, "The Populist Heritage and the Intellectual," American Scholar (Winter 1959–60). Reprinted by permission of the author.

American historiography of the 1930s and 1940s reflects a strong persuasion of this sort. The most popular college textbook in American history was written by a Midwesterner who was friendly to Populism and was himself the foremost historian of the movement. The leading competitor among textbooks shared many of the Populist leanings, even though one of its authors was a Harvard patrician and the other a Columbia urbanite. A remarkably heterogeneous assortment struck up congenial ties in the neo-Populist coalition. Small-town Southerners and big-city Northerners, Texas mavericks and Hudson River aristocrats, Chapel Hill liberals and Nashville agrarians were all able to discover some sort of identity in the heritage. The South rediscovered ties with the West, the farmer with labor. The New York-Virginia axis was revived. Jacksonians were found to have urban affiliations and origins. Not to be outdone, the Communists staked out claims to selected Populist heroes.

Many intellectuals made themselves at home in the neo-Populist coalition and embraced the Populist heritage. They had prepared the way for the affiliation in the twenties when they broke with the genteel tradition, adopted the mucker pose, and decided that conventional politics and the two major parties were the province of the boobocracy and that professional politicians were clowns or hypocrites. In the thirties intellectuals made naive identification with farmers and workers and supported their spokesmen with enthusiasm. The Populist affinity outlasted the New Deal, survived the war, and perhaps found its fullest expression in the spirit of indulgent affection with which intellectuals often supported Harry Truman and his administration.

Hardly had Truman left the White House, however, when the Populist identification fell into disgrace and intellectuals began to repudiate the heritage. "Populist" suddenly became a term of opprobrium, in some circles a pejorative epithet. This resulted from no transfer of affection to Truman's successor, for there was very little of that among intellectuals. It resulted instead from the shock of the encounter with McCarthyism. Liberals and intellectuals bore the brunt of the degrading McCarthyite assault upon standards of decency. They were rightly alarmed and felt themselves betrayed. Something had gone badly wrong. They were the victims of a perversion of the democracy they cherished, a seamy and sinister side of democracy to which they now guiltily realized they had all along tended to turn a blind or indulgent eye. Stung by consciousness of their own negligence or naiveté, they reacted with a healthy impulse to make up for lost time and to confront their problem boldly with all the critical resources at their command. The consequence has been a formidable and often valuable corpus of social criticism.

Not one of the critics, not even the most conservative, is prepared to repudiate democracy. There is general agreement that the fault lay in some abuse or perversion of democracy, and was not inherent in democracy itself. All the critics are aware that these abuses and perversions had historic antecedents and had appeared in various guises and with disturbing frequency in national history. These unhappy tendencies are variously described as "mobism," "direct democracy," or "plebiscitarianism," but there is a surprising and apparently spontaneous consensus of preference for "Populism." Although the word is usually capitalized, most of the critics do not limit its reference to the political party that gave currency to the term. While there is general agreement that the essential characteristics designated by the term are best illustrated by an agrarian movement in the last decade of the nineteenth century, some of the critics take the liberty of applying it to movements as early as the Jacksonians, or earlier, and to twentieth century phenomena as well.

The reasons for this convergence from several angles upon "Populism" as the appropriate designation for an abhorred abuse are not all clear. A few, however, suggest themselves. Populism is generally thought of as an entirely Western affair, Wisconsin as a seedbed of the movement, and Old Bob La Follette as a foremost exponent. None of these assumptions is historically warranted, but it is true that Senator McCarthy came from Wisconsin, that much of his support came from the Middle West, and that there are some similarities between the two movements. The impression of similarity has been enhanced by the historical echo of their own alarm that modern intellectuals have caught in the rather hysterical fright with which Eastern conservatives reacted to Populism in the nineties.

This essay is not concerned with the validity of recent analysis of the "radical right" and its fascistic manifestations in America. It is concerned only with the tendency to identify Populism with these movements and with the implied rejection of the Populist tradition. It is admittedly very difficult, without risk of misrepresentation and injustice, to generalize about the way in which numerous critics have

employed the Populist identification. They differ widely in the meaning they attribute to the term and the importance they attach to the
identification. Among the critics are sociologists, political scientists,
poets and journalists, as well as historians, and there is naturally a
diversity in the degree of historical awareness and competence they
command. Among points of view represented are the New Conservative, the New Liberal, the liberal-progressive, the Jewish, the Anglo-
phile, and the urban, with some overlapping. There are no conscious
spokesmen of the West or the South, but some are more-or-less
conscious representatives of the urban East. Every effort will be
made not to attribute to one the view of another.

Certain concessions are due at the outset. Any fair-minded historian will acknowledge the validity of some of the points scored by
the new critics against the Populist tradition and its defenses. It is
undoubtedly true that liberal intellectuals have in the past con-
structed a flattering image of Populism. They have permitted their
sympathy with oppressed groups to blind them to the delusions,
myths, and foibles of the people with whom they sympathized. Sharing certain political and economic doctrines and certain indignations
with the Populists, they have attributed to them other values, tastes
and principles that the Populists did not actually profess. It was
understandably distasteful to dwell upon the irrational or retrograde
traits of people who deserved one's sympathy and shared some of
one's views. For undertaking this neglected and distasteful task in
the spirit of civility and forbearance which, for example, Richard
Hofstadter has shown, some of the new critics deserve much credit.
All of them concede some measure of value in the Populist heritage,
although none so handsomely as Hofstadter, who assumes that
Populism and Progressivism are strongly enough established in our
tradition to withstand criticism. Others are prone to make their concessions more perfunctory and to hasten on with the job of heaping
upon Populism, as upon a historical scapegoat, all the ills to which
democracy is heir.

The danger is that under the concentrated impact of the new
criticism the risk is incurred not only of blurring a historical image
but of swapping an old stereotype for a new one. The old one sometimes approached the formulation that Populism is the root of all
good in democracy, while the new one sometimes suggests that
Populism is the root of all evil. Uncritical repetition and occasional

exaggeration of the strictures of some of the critics threaten to result in establishing a new maxim in American political thought: *Radix malorum est Populismus.*

Few of the critics engaged in the reassessment of Populism and the analysis of the New American Right would perhaps go quite so far as Peter Viereck, when he writes, "Beneath the sane economic demands of the Populists of 1880–1900 seethed a mania for xenophobia, Jew-baiting, intellectual-baiting, and thought-controlling lynch-spirit." Yet this far from exhausts the list of unhappy or repulsive aberrations of the American spirit that have been attributed to Populism. Other aberrations are not pictured as a "seething mania" by any one critic, but by one or another the Populists are charged with some degree of responsibility for Anglophobia, Negrophobia, isolationism, imperialism, jingoism, paranoidal conspiracy-hunting, anti-constitutionalism, anti-intellectualism, and the assault upon the right of privacy, among others. The Populist virus is seen as no respecter of the barriers of time or nationality. According to Edward A. Shils, "populism has many faces. Nazi dictatorship had markedly populistic features. . . . Bolshevism has a strand of populism in it too. . . ." And there was among fellow travelers a "populistic predisposition to Stalinism." On the domestic scene the strand of populistic tradition "is so powerful that it influences reactionaries like McCarthy and left-wing radicals and great upperclass personalities like Franklin Roosevelt." And according to Viereck, populistic attitudes once "underlay Robespierre's Committee of Public Safety" and later "our neo-Populist Committee on Un-American Activities."

Among certain of the critics there is no hesitancy in finding a direct continuity between the nineteenth-century Populists and twentieth-century American fascism and McCarthyism. Victor C. Ferkiss states flatly that "American fascism has its roots in American populism. It pursued the same ends and even used many of the same slogans. Both despaired of achieving a just society under the joined banners of liberalism and capitalism." His assertion supports Viereck's suggestion that "since the same impulses and resentments inspire the old Populism and the new nationalist right, let us adopt 'neo-Populism' as the proper term for the latter group." Talcott Parsons believes that "the elements of continuity between Western agrarian populism and McCarthyism are not by any means purely fortuitous," and Edward Shils thinks the two are connected by "a straight line." It remained for Viereck to fill in the gap: "The missing link between the Populism of 1880–1900 and the neo-Populism of today—the missing link between Ignatius Donnelly and the McCarthy movement—was Father Charles Coughlin."

There is a strong tendency among the critics not only to identify Populism and the New Radical Right, but to identify both with certain regions, the West and South, and particularly the Middle West. "The areas which produced the populism of the end of the nineteenth century and the early twentieth century have continued to produce them," writes Shils. Viereck puts it somewhat more colorfully: "The Bible-belt of Fundamentalism in religion mostly overlapped with the farm-belt of the Populist, Greenback, and other free-silver parties in politics. Both belts were anti-intellectual, anti-aristocratic, anti-capitalist." Talcott Parsons and Ferkiss likewise stress the regional identity of Populist-Radical Right ideology, and Viereck supplies an interesting illustration: "Out of the western Populist movement came such apostles of thought-control and racist bigotry as Tom Watson. . . ."

If so many undesirable traits are conveniently concentrated along geographical lines, it might serve a useful purpose to straighten out the political geography of Populism a bit. In the first place, as Hofstadter and other historians of the movement have noted, Populism had negligible appeal in the Middle Western states, and so did the quasi-Populism of William Jennings Bryan. Wisconsin, Minnesota, Iowa, Illinois and states east of them went down the line for McKinley, Hanna, gold and the Old Conservatism (and so did Old Bob La Follette). Only in the plains states of the Dakotas, Nebraska and Kansas were there strong Populist leanings, and only they and the mountain states went for Bryan in 1896. At the crest of the Populist wave in 1894 only Nebraska polled a Populist vote comparable in strength to that run up in Alabama, Georgia, and North Carolina.

For the dubious distinction of being the leading Populist section, the South is in fact a strong contender; and if the test is merely quasi-Populism, the preeminence of the former Confederacy is unchallengeable. It was easily the most solidly Bryan section of the country, and its dogged loyalty far outlasted that of the Nebraskan's native state. But a more important test was third-party Populism, the genuine article. The remarkable strength the Populists manifested in the Lower South was gained against far more formidable obstacles than any ever encountered in the West. For there they daily faced the implacable dogmas of racism, white solidarity, white supremacy and the bloody shirt. There was indeed plenty of "thought-control and racist bigotry and lynch-spirit," but the Populists were far more often the victims than the perpetrators. They had to contend regularly with foreclosure of mortgages, discharge from jobs, eviction as tenants, exclusion from church, withholding of credit, boycott, social ostracism and the endlessly reiterated charge of racial disloyalty and sectional disloyalty. Suspicion of loyalty was in fact *the* major psychological problem of the Southern Populists, as much so perhaps as the problem of loyalty faced by radicals of today. They contended also against cynical use of fraud comparable with any used against Reconstruction, methods that included stuffed ballot boxes, packed courts, stacked registration and election boards, and open bribery. They saw election after election stolen from them and heard their opponents boast of the theft. They were victims of mobs and lynchers. Some fifteen Negroes and several white men were killed in the Georgia Populist campaign of 1892, and it was rare that a major election in the Lower South came off without casualties.

Having waged their revolt at such great cost, the Southern Populists were far less willing to compromise their principles than were their Western brethren. It was the Western Populists who planned and led the movement to sell out the party to the silverites, and the Southern Populists who fought and resisted the drift to quasi-Populism. The Southerners were consistently more radical, more insistent upon their economic reforms, and more stubbornly unwilling to lose their party identity in the watered-down populism of Bryan than were Western Populists.

There is some lack of understanding about *who* the Southern Populists were for and against, as well as *what* they were for and against. Edward Shils writes that the "economic and political feebleness and pretensions to breeding and culture" of the "older aristocratic ruling class" in the South provided "a fertile ground for populistic denunciation of the upper classes." Actually the Southern Populists directed their rebellion against the newer ruling class, the industrialists and businessmen of the New South instead of the old planters. A few of the quasi-Populists like Ben Tillman did divert resentment to aristocrats like Wade Hampton. But the South was still a more deferential society than the rest of the country, and the Populists were as ready as the railroads and insurance companies to borrow the prestige and name of a great family. The names of the Populist officials in Virginia sounded like a roll call of colonial assemblies or Revolutionary founding fathers: Page, Cocke, Harrison, Beverly, Ruffin. There were none more aristocratic in the Old Dominion. General Robert E. Lee, after the surrender at Appomattox, retired to the ancestral home of Edmund Randolph Cocke after his labors. His host was later Populist candidate for governor of the state. As the editor of their leading paper, the allegedly Anglophobic Populists of Virginia chose Charles H. Pierson, an ordained Anglican priest, English by birth, Cambridge graduate and theological student of Oxford. To be sure, the Populist leaders of Virginia were not typical of the movement in the South. But neither were Jefferson, Madison, Monroe, and John Taylor typical of *their* movement in the South: there were never enough aristocrats to go around. Some states had to make do with cruder customers as leaders in both Jeffersonian and Populist movements, and in the states to the west there doubtless was less habitual dependence on aristocrats even if they had been more readily available.

In their analysis of the radical right of modern America, the new critics have made use of the concept of "status resentment" as the political motivation of their subjects. They distinguish between "class politics," which has to do with the correction of economic deprivations, and "status politics," which has no definite solutions and no clear-cut legislative program but responds to irrational appeals and vents aggression and resentment for status insecurity upon scapegoats—usually ethnic minorities. Seymour Martin Lipset, who appears at times to include Populism in the category, has outlined the conditions typical of periods when status politics become ascendant. These are, he writes, "periods of prosperity, especially when full employment is accompanied by inflation, and when many individuals are able to improve their economic position." But the conditions under which Populism rose were exactly the opposite: severe depression, critical unemployment and crippling currency contraction, when few were able to improve their economic position—and certainly not farmers in cash-crop staple agriculture.

The Populists may have been bitten by status anxieties, but if so they were certainly not bred of upward social mobility, and probably few by downward mobility either—for the simple reason that there was not much further downward for most Populists to go, and had not been for some time. Populism was hardly "status politics," and I should hesitate to call it "class politics." It was more nearly "interest politics," and more specifically "agricultural interest politics." Whatever concern the farmers might have had for their status was overwhelmed by desperate and immediate economic anxieties. Not only their anxieties but their proposed solutions and remedies were economic. While their legislative program may have been often naive and inadequate, it was almost obsessively economic and, as political platforms go, little more irrational than the run of the mill.

Yet one of the most serious charges leveled against the Populists in the reassessment by the new critics is an addiction to just the sort of irrational obsession that is typical of status politics. This is the charge of anti-Semitism. It has been documented most fully by Richard Hofstadter and Oscar Handlin and advanced less critically by others. The prejudice is attributed to characteristic Populist traits —rural provinciality, and ominous credulity and an obsessive fascination with conspiracy. Baffled by the complexities of monetary and banking problems, Populist ideologues simplified them into a rural melodrama with Jewish international bankers as the principal villains. Numerous writings of Western Populists are cited that illustrate the tendency to use Jewish financiers and their race as scapegoats for agrarian resentment. Hofstadter points out that Populist anti-Semitism was entirely verbal and rhetorical and cautions that it can easily be misconstrued and exaggerated. Nevertheless, he is of the opinion "that the Greenback-Populist tradition activated most of what we have of modern popular anti-Semitism in the United States."

In the voluminous literature of the nineties on currency and monetary problems—problems that were much more stressed by silverites and quasi-Populists than by radical Populists—three symbols were repetitively used for the plutocratic adversary. One was institutional, Wall Street; and two were ethnic, the British and Jewish bankers. Wall Street was by far the most popular and has remained so ever since among politicians of agrarian and Populistic tradition. Populist agitators used the ethnic symbols more or less indiscriminately, British along with Jewish, although some of them bore down with peculiar viciousness on the Semitic symbol. As the new critics have pointed out, certain Eastern intellectuals of the patrician sort, such as Henry and Brooks Adams and Henry Cabot Lodge, shared the Populist suspicion and disdain of the plutocracy and likewise shared their rhetorical anti-Semitism. John Higham has called attention to a third anti-Semitic group of the nineties, the poorer classes in urban centers. Their prejudice cannot be described as merely verbal and rhetorical. Populists were not responsible for a protest signed by fourteen Jewish societies in 1899 that "No Jew can go on the street without exposing himself to the danger of being pitilessly beaten." That was in Brooklyn. And the mob of 1902 that injured some two hundred people, mostly Jewish, went into action in Lower East Side New York.

Populist anti-Semitism is not to be excused on the ground that it was verbal, nor dismissed because the prejudice received more violent expression in urban quarters. But all would admit that the charge of anti-Semitism has taken on an infinitely more ominous and hideous significance since the Nazi genocide furnaces than it ever had before, at least in Anglo-American society. The Populists' use of the Shylock symbol was not wholly innocent, but they used it as a folk stereotype, and little had happened in the Anglo-Saxon community between the time of Shakespeare and that of the Populists that burdened the latter with additional guilt in repeating the stereotype.

The South, again, was a special instance. Much had happened there to enhance the guilt of racist propaganda and to exacerbate racism. But anti-Semitism was not the trouble, and to stress it in connection with the South of the nineties would be comparable to stressing anti-Negro feeling in the Arab states of the Middle East today. Racism there was, in alarming quantity, but it was directed against another race and it was not merely rhetorical. The Negro suffered far more discrimination and violence than the Jew did in that era or later. Moreover, there was little in the Southern tradition to restrain the political exploitation of anti-Negro prejudice and much more to encourage its use than there was in the American tradition with respect to anti-Semitism. Racism was exploited in the South with fantastic refinements and revolting excesses in the Populist period. Modern students of the dynamics of race prejudice, such as Bruno Bettelheim and Morris Janowitz, find similarities between anti-Negro feelings and anti-Semitism and in the psychological traits of those to whom both appeal. First in the list of those traits under both anti-Negro attitudes and anti-Semitism is "the feeling of deprivation," and another lower in the list but common to both, is "economic apprehensions." The Southern Populists would seem to have constituted the perfect market for Negrophobia.

But perhaps the most remarkable aspect of the whole Populist movement was the resistance its leaders in the South put up against racism and racist propaganda and the determined effort they made against incredible odds to win back political rights for the Negroes, to defend those rights against brutal aggression, and to create among their normally anti-Negro following, even temporarily, a spirit of tolerance in which the two races of the South could work together in one party for the achievement of common ends. These efforts included not only the defense of the Negro's right to vote, but also his right to hold office, serve on juries, receive justice in the courts and defense against lynchers. The Populists failed, and some of them turned bitterly against the Negro as the cause of their failure. But in the efforts they made for racial justice and political rights they went further toward extending the Negro political fellowship, recognition and equality than any native white political movement has ever gone before or since in the South. This record is of greater historical significance and deserves more emphasis and attention than any anti-Semitic tendencies the movement manifested in that region or any other. If resistance to racism is the test of acceptability for a place in the American political heritage, Populism would seem to deserve more indulgence at the hands of its critics than it has recently enjoyed.

Two other aspects of the identification between the old Populism and the new radical right require critical modification. Talcott Parsons, Max Lerner, and Victor Ferkiss, among others, find that the old regional strongholds of Populism tended to become the strongholds of isolationism in the period between the two world wars and believe there is more than a fortuitous connection between a regional proneness to Populism and isolationism. These and other critics believe also that they discern a logical connection between a regional addiction to Populism in the old days and to McCarthyism in recent times.

In both of these hypotheses the critics have neglected to take into account the experience of the South and mistakenly assumed a strong Populist heritage in the Middle West. One of the strongest centers of Populism, if not the strongest, the South in the foreign

policy crisis before the Second World War, was the least isolationist
and the most internationalist and interventionist part of the country.
And after the war, according to Nathan Glazer and Seymour Lipset,
who base their statement on opinion poll studies, "the South was the
most anti-McCarthy section of the country." It is perfectly possible
that in rejecting isolationism and McCarthyism the South was "right"
for the "wrong" reasons, traditional and historical reasons. V. O. Key
has suggested that among the reasons for its position on foreign
policy were centuries of dependence on world trade, the absence of
any concentration of Irish or Germanic population, and the predominantly British origin of the white population. Any adequate
explanation of the South's rejection of McCarthy would be complex,
but part of it might be the region's peculiarly rich historical experience with its own assortment of demagogues—Populistic and other
varieties—and the consequent acquirement of some degree of sophistication and some minimal standards of decency in the arts of
demagoguery. No one has attempted to explain the South's anti-
isolationism and anti-McCarthyism by reference to its Populist heritage—and certainly no such explanation is advanced here.

To do justice to the new critique of Populism it should be acknowledged that much of its bill of indictment is justified. It is true
that the Populists were a provincial lot and that much of their thinking was provincial. It is true that they took refuge in the agrarian
myth, that they denied the commercial character of agricultural enterprise and sometimes dreamed of a Golden Age. In their economic
thought they overemphasized the importance of money and over-
simplified the nature of their problems by claiming a harmony of
interest between farmer and labor, by dividing the world into "producers" and "nonproducers," by reducing all conflict to "just two
sides," and by thinking that too many ills and too many remedies of
the world were purely legislative. Undoubtedly many of them were
fascinated with the notion of conspiracy and advanced conspiratorial theories of history, and some of them were given to apocalyptic premonitions of direful portent.

To place these characteristics in perspective, however, one should
inquire how many of them are peculiar to the Populists and how
many are shared by the classes or groups or regions or by the
period to which the Populists belong. The great majority of Populists were provincial, ill-educated and rural, but so were the great

majority of Americans in the nineties, Republicans and Democrats as well. They were heirs to all the superstition, folklore and prejudice that is the heritage of the ill-informed. The Populists utilized and institutionalized some of this, but so did their opponents. There were a good many conspiratorial theories and economic nostrums and oversimplifications adrift in the latter part of the nineteenth century, and the Populists had no monopoly of them. They did overemphasize the importance of money, but scarcely more so than did their opponents, the Gold Bugs. The preoccupation with monetary reforms and remedies was a characteristic of the period rather than a peculiarity of the Populists. The genuine Populist, moreover, was more concerned with the "primacy of credit" than with the "primacy of money," and his insistence that the federal government was the only agency powerful enough to provide a solution for the agricultural credit problem proved to be sound. And so did his contention that the banking system was stacked against his interest and that reform in this field was overdue.

The Populist doctrine of a harmony of interest between farmer and labor, between workers and small businessmen, and the alignment of these "producers" against the parasitic "nonproducers," is not without precedent in our political history. Any party that aspires to gain power in America must strive for a coalition of conflicting interest groups. The Populist effort was no more irrational in this respect than was the Whig coalition and many others, including the New Deal coalition.

The political crises of the nineties evoked hysterical responses and apocalyptic delusions in more than one quarter. The excesses of the leaders of a protest movement of provincial, unlettered, and angry farmers are actually more excusable and understandable than the rather similar responses of the spokesmen of the educated, successful, and privileged classes of the urban East. There would seem to be less excuse for hysteria and conspiratorial obsessions among the latter. One thinks of the *Nation* describing the Sherman Silver Purchase Act as a "socialistic contrivance of gigantic proportions," or of Police Commissioner Theodore Roosevelt declaring in "the greatest soberness" that the Populists were "plotting a social revolution and the subversion of the American Republic" and proposing to make an example of twelve of their leaders by "shooting them dead" against a wall. Or there was Joseph H. Choate before the

Supreme Court pronouncing the income tax "the beginnings of socialism and Communism" and "the destruction of the Constitution itself." For violence of rhetoric *Harper's Weekly,* the *New York Tribune* and the *Springfield Republican* could hold their own with the wool-hat press in the campaign of 1896. Hysteria was not confined to mugwump intellectuals with status problems. Mark Hanna told an assembly of his wealthy friends at the Union League Club they were acting like "a lot of scared hens."

Anarchism was almost as much a conspiracy symbol of conservatives as Wall Street was for the Populists, and conservatives responded to any waving of the symbol even more irrationally, for there was less reality in the menace of anarchism for capitalism. John Hay had a vituperative address called "The Platform of Anarchy" that he used in the campaign of 1896. The *Springfield Republican* called Bryan "the exaltation of anarchy"; Dr. Lyman Abbott labeled Bryanites "the anarchists of the Northwest," and Dr. Charles H. Parkhurst was excited about the menace of "anarchism" in the Democratic platform. It was the Populist sympathizer Governor John Peter Altgeld of Illinois who pardoned the three anarchists of Haymarket, victims of conservative hysteria, and partly corrected the gross miscarriage of justice that had resulted in the hanging of four others. The *New York Times* promptly denounced Governor Altgeld as a secret anarchist himself, and Theodore Roosevelt said that Altgeld would conspire to inaugurate "a red government of lawlessness and dishonesty as fantastic and vicious as the Paris Commune." There was more than a touch of conspiratorial ideology in the desperate conservative reaction to the agrarian revolt. An intensive study of the nineties can hardly fail to leave the impression that this decade had rather more than its share of zaniness and crankiness, and that these qualities were manifested in the higher and middling as well as the lower orders of American society.

Venturing beyond the 1890s and speaking of populists with a small *p,* some of the new critics would suggest that popular protest movements of the populistic style throughout our history have suffered from a peculiar addiction to scares, scapegoats, and conspiratorial notions. It is true that such movements tend to attract the less sophisticated, the people who are likely to succumb to cranks and the appeal of their menaces and conspiratorial obsessions. But before one accepts this as a populistic or radical peculiarity, one should recall that the Jacobin Scare of the 1790s was a Federalist crusade and that the populistic elements of that era were its victims and not its perpetrators. One should remember also that A. Mitchell Palmer and the superpatriots who staged the Great Red Scare of 1919–20 were not populistic in their outlook. One of the most successful conspiratorial theories of history in American politics was the Great Slave Conspiracy notion advanced by the abolitionists and later incorporated in the Republican party credo for several decades.

Richard Hofstadter has put his finger on a neglected tendency of some Populists and Progressives as well, the tendency he calls "deconversion from reform to reaction," the tendency to turn cranky, illiberal and sour. This happend with disturbing frequency among leaders as well as followers of Populism. Perhaps the classic example is the Georgia Populist Tom Watson, twice his party's candidate for president and once for vice-president. When Watson soured he went the whole way. By no means all of the Populist leaders turned sour, but there are several other valid instances. Even more disturbing is the same tendency to turn sour among the old Populist rank and file, to take off after race phobias, religious hatreds, and witch hunts. The reasons for this retrograde tendency among reformers to embrace the forces they have spent years in fighting have not been sufficiently investigated. It may be that in some instances the reform movement appeals to personalities with unstable psychological traits. In the case of the Populists, however, it would seem that a very large part of the explanation lies in embittered frustration—repeated and tormenting frustration of both the leaders and the led.

Whatever the explanation, it cannot be denied that some of the offshoots of Populism are less than lovely to contemplate and rather painful to recall. Misshapen and sometimes hideous, they are caricatures of the Populist ideal, although their kinship with the genuine article is undeniable. No one in his right mind can glory in their memory, and it would at times be a welcome relief to renounce the whole Populist heritage in order to be rid of the repulsive aftermath. Repudiation of the Populist tradition presents the liberal-minded Southerner in particular with a temptation of no inconsiderable appeal, for it would unburden him of a number of embarrassing associations.

In his study of populist traits in American society, Edward Shils has some perceptive observations on the difficult relations between politicians and intellectuals. He adds a rather wistful footnote: "How painful the American situation looked to our intellectuals when they thought of Great Britain. There the cream of the graduates of the two ancient universities entered the civil service by examinations which were delightfully archaic and which had no trace of spoils patronage about them. . . . Politics, radical politics, conducted in a seemly fashion by the learned and reflective was wonderful. It was an ideal condition which was regretfully recognized as impossible to reproduce in the United States," He himself points out many of the reasons why this is possible in Britain, the most dignified member of the parliamentary fraternity: respect for "betters," mutual trust within the ruling classes, deferential attitudes of working class and middle class, the aura of aristocracy and monarchy that still suffuses the institutions of a government no longer artistocratic, the retention of the status and the symbols of hierarchy despite economic leveling. No wonder that from some points of view, "the British system seemed an intellectual's paradise."

America has it worse—or at least different. The differential attitude lingers only in the South, and there mainly as a quaint gesture of habit. Respect for "betters" is un-American. Glaring publicity replaces mutual trust as the *modus vivendi* among the political elite. No aura of aristocratic decorum and hierarchal sanctity surrounds our governmental institutions, even the most august of them. Neither Supreme Court nor State Department nor Army is immune from popular assault and the rude hand of suspicion. The sense of institutional identity is weak, and so are institutional loyalties. Avenues between the seats of learning and the seats of power are often blocked by mistrust and mutual embarrassment.

America has no reason to expect that it could bring off a social revolution without a breach of decorum or the public peace, nor that the revolutionary party would eventually be led by a graduate of exclusive Winchester and Oxford. American politics are not ordinarily "conducted in a seemly fashion by the learned and reflective." Such success as we have enjoyed in this respect—the instances of the Sage of Monticello and the aristocrat of Hyde Park come to mind —have to be accounted for by a large element of luck. Close investigation of popular upheavals of protest and reform in the political history of the United States has increasingly revealed of late that they have all had their seamy side and their share of the irrational, the zany, and the retrograde. A few of the more successful movements have borrowed historical reputability from the memory of the worthies who led them, but others have not been so fortunate either in their leaders or their historians.

One must expect and even hope that there will be future upheavals to shock the seats of power and privilege and furnish the periodic therapy that seems necessary to the health of our democracy. But one cannot expect them to be any more decorous or seemly or rational than their predecessors. One can reasonably hope, however, that they will not all fall under the sway of the Huey Longs and Father Coughlins who will be ready to take charge. Nor need they if the tradition is maintained which enabled a Henry George to place himself in the vanguard of the antimonopoly movement in his day, which encouraged a Henry Demarest Lloyd to labor valiantly to shape the course of Populism, or which prompted an Upton Sinclair to try to make sense of a rag-tag-and-bob-tail aberration in California.

For the tradition to endure, for the way to remain open, however, the intellectual must not be alienated from the sources of revolt. It was one of the glories of the New Deal that it won the support of the intellectual and one of the tragedies of Populism that it did not. The intellectual must resist the impulse to identify all the irrational and evil forces he detests with such movements because some of them, or the aftermath or epigone of some of them, have proved so utterly repulsive. He will learn all he can from the new criticism about the irrational and illiberal side of Populism and other reform movements, but he cannot afford to repudiate the heritage.

Sociological Critiques

Daniel Bell
STATUS POLITICS AND NEW ANXIETIES

Daniel Bell, formerly managing editor of the New Leader, *and a member of the sociology faculty of Columbia University, is now a member of the sociology faculty at Harvard University.*

Granting the viability of [these] conventional lines of political analysis—the role of the two-party system in limiting social movements and social clashes, the political tradition of direct appeal to the people, and the force of interest groups in shaping and modifying legislative policy—they nevertheless leave us somewhat ill-equipped to understand the issues which have dominated the politics of the 1950s decade. These lines of thought do not help us, for example, to understand the Communist issue, the forces behind the new nationalism of, say, Senators Bricker and Knowland, and the momentary range of support and intense emotional heat generated by Senator McCarthy. In short, what has traditionally been called "interest-group" politics does not help to explain the emergence of the new American right wing, the group that S. M. Lipset has dubbed the "radical right"—radical because it opposes traditional conservatism, with its respect for individual rights, and because it sought to impose new patterns in American life. All this is dramatized by the issue of McCarthy and the Communists.

For Europeans, particularly, the Communist issue must be a puzzle. After all, there is no mass Communist party in the United States such as one finds in France and Italy; the Communist party in the U.S. never, at any single moment, had more than 100,000 members. In the last five years, when the Communist issue entered the national scene, the Communists had already lost most of the political influence they once had. The Communist unions had been expelled from the CIO;

the Progressive party, repudiated by Henry Wallace, had fizzled; and they were fast losing strength in the intellectual community.

It is true that liberals have tended to play down the Communist issue. And the contradictory stand of the Truman administration compounded these confusions and increased the alarms: on the one hand, leading members of the administration, including Truman himself, sought to minimize the degree of past Communist infiltration; on the other hand, the administration let loose a buckshot charge of security regulations which had little regard for personal liberties and rights. The invasion of South Korea and the emotional reaction against the Chinese and Russian Communists, which carried over to domestic Communists; the disclosures, particularly by Whittaker Chambers, of the infiltration of Communists into high posts in government and the existence of espionage rings; and, finally, the revelations in the Canadian spy investigations, in the Allan Nunn May trial in Britain, and in the Rosenberg case that the Soviets had stolen U.S. atom secrets, all played a role in heightening national tension.

But even after the natural effects of all these are taken into account, it is difficult to explain the unchallenged position so long held by Senator McCarthy. It still fails to take into account the extensive damage to the democratic fabric that McCarthy and others were able to cause on the Communist issue, as well as the reckless methods disproportionate to the problem: the loyalty oaths on campuses, the compulsive Americanism which saw threats to the country in the wording of a Girl Scout handbook, the violent clubbing of the Voice of America (which under the sensible leadership of anti-Communists, such as Bertram D. Wolfe, had conducted intelligent propaganda in Europe), the wild headlines and the senseless damaging of the Signal Corps radar research program at Fort Monmouth—in short, the suspicion and miasma of fear that played so large a role in American politics. Nor can conventional political analysis shed much light on him or his supporters. Calling him a demagogue explains little; the relevant questions arise in relation to whom and what he was demagogic about. McCarthy's targets were indeed strange. Huey Long, the last major demagogue, had vaguely attacked the rich and sought to "share the wealth." McCarthy's targets were intellectuals, especially Harvard men, Anglophiles, internationalists, the army.

But these targets provide the important clues to the right-wing support, a "radical right," that backed him, and the reasons for that support. These groups constituted a strange mélange: a thin stratum of soured patricians like Archibald Roosevelt, the last surviving son of Theodore Roosevelt, whose emotional stake lay in a vanishing image of a muscular American defying a decadent Europe; the "new rich"—the automobile dealers, real estate manipulators, oil wildcatters—who needed the psychological assurance that they, like their forebears, had earned their own wealth, rather than (as in fact) through government aid, and who feared that "taxes" would rob them of that wealth; the rising middle-class strata of the various ethnic groups, especially the Irish and the Germans, who sought to prove their Americanism (the Germans particularly because of the implied taint of disloyalty during World War II); and, finally, unique in U.S. cultural history, a small group of intellectuals, some of them cankered ex-Communists, who, pivoting on McCarthy, opened up an attack on liberalism in general.

If this strange coalition, bearing the "sword of the Lord and Gideon," cannot be explained in the conventional terms that are applied to American politics," what can? One key concept is the idea of "status politics," an idea which has been used by Richard Hofstadter to deal with the status anxieties of the old aristocracy, and by S. M. Lipset with the status fears of the new rich.

The central idea of the status politics conception is that groups that are advancing in wealth and social position are often as anxious and politically feverish as groups that have become *déclassé*. Many observers have noted that those groups which have lost their social position seek more violently than ever to impose on all groups the older values of a society which they once represented. Lipset has demonstrated that groups on the rise, in order to establish themselves, may insist on a similar conformity. This rise takes place in periods of prosperity, when class or economic interest-group conflicts have lost much of their force. And Hofstadter has argued further that economic issues take on importance in American political history only during the depressions, while in periods of prosperity "status" issues emerge. But these issues, usually "patriotic" in character, are amorphous and ideological.

These political forces, by their very nature, are unstable. McCarthy himself, by the logic of his own political position, and by the nature of his personality, had to go to an extreme. And he ended, finally, by challenging Eisenhower. It was McCarthy's great gamble.

And he lost, for the challenge to a Republican president by a Republican minority could only have split the party. Faced with this threat, the party rallied behind Eisenhower, and McCarthy himself was isolated. In this respect, the events prove the soundness of the thesis of Walter Lippmann and the Alsops in 1952 that only a Republican president could provide the necessary continuity of foreign and domestic policy initiated and maintained by the Fair Deal. A Democratic president might have polarized the parties and given the extreme Republican wing the license to lead the attack; the administration of a moderate Republican could act as a damper on the extreme right.

The lessening of international tensions after the settlement in Korea confirmed McCarthy's defeat. Yet McCarthy has to be understood in relation to the people behind him and the changed political temper which these groups have brought. He was the catalyst, not the explosive force. These forces still remain.

There are several consequences to the changed political temper in American life, most notably the introduction on a large scale of "moral issues" into political debate. By and large, this is new. Throughout their history, Americans have had an extraordinary talent for compromise in politics and extremism in morality.

The saving grace, so to speak, of American politics, was that all sorts of groups were tolerated, and the system of the "deal" became the pragmatic counterpart of the philosophic principle of toleration. But in matters of manners, morals, and conduct—particularly in the small towns—there has been a ferocity of blue-nose attitudes unmatched by other countries.

The sources of this moralism are varied. This has been a middle-class culture, and there is much truth to the generalization of Max Scheler that moral indignation is a disguised form of repressed envy and a peculiar fact of middle-class psychology. In aristocratic cultures, with their free-and-easy ways, with their search for pleasure and their concentration on aestheticism, one rarely finds moral indignation an aspect of their temper. Some Catholic cultures, worldly in their wisdom and tolerant of human frailties, do not look with horror at gambling, drink, or even easy sexual conduct; disapproval is tempered with a sense of the inevitability of sin, and salvation is of the other world, not this; theft after all is a venial disgrace, but pride bears the strain of the mortal sin.

Moral indignation—and moralism—are characteristic of religions that have abandoned otherworldly preoccupations and concentrate on this-worldly concerns. In Protestantism, such a displacement finds piety giving way to moralism, and theology to ethics. Becoming respectable represents "moral" advancement, and regulating conduct, i.e., being "moral" about it, has been a great concern of the Protestant churches of America.

This moralism, itself not unique to America, is linked to an evangelicism that is unique. There has long been a legend, fostered for the most part by literary people, and compounded by sociologists, that America's has been a "puritan" culture. For the sociologists this has arisen out of a mistaken identification of the Protestant ethic with the Puritan code. Puritanism and the "New England mind" have played a large intellectual role in American life. But in the habits and mores of the masses of the people, the peculiar evangelicism of Methodism and Baptism, with its high emotionalism, its fervor, enthusiasm, and excitement, its revivalism, its excesses of sinning and of high-voltage confessing, has played a much more important role. Baptism and Methodism have been the favorite American religious creeds, because they were the rustic and frontier religions. In his page on "Why Americans Manifest a Sort of Fanatical Spiritualism," Alexis de Tocqueville observed: "In all states of the Union, but especially in the half-peopled country of the Far West, itinerant preachers may be met with who hawk about the word of God from place to place. Whole families, old men, women and children, cross rough passes and untrodden wilds, coming from a great distance, to join a camp meeting, where, in listening to these discourses, they totally forget for several days and nights the cares of business and even the most urgent wants of the body."

The Baptist and Methodist churches grew, while the more "respectable" Protestant bodies remained static, precisely because their preachers moved with the advancing frontier and reflected its spirit. "In the camp-meeting and in the political gathering logical discourse was of no avail, while the 'language of excitement' called forth an enthusiastic response," H. Richard Niebuhr has observed.

The revivalist spirit was egalitarian and anti-intellectual. It shook off the vestments and the formal liturgies and preached instead the gospel and roaring hymn. This evangelicism was reflected in the moralism of a William Jennings Bryan, a religious as well as economic champion of the West, and in the urban revivalism of a Dwight Moody and the YMCA movement that grew out of his gospel fervor. The evangelical churches wanted to "improve" man, whereas the liberals wanted to reform institutions. The former were the supreme champions of prohibition legislation and Sabbath observance. *Reform in their terms meant not a belief in welfare legislation but in the redemption of those who had fallen prey to sin*—and sin meant drink, loose women, and gambling.

This moralism, so characteristic of the American temper, had a peculiar schizoid character: it would be imposed with vehemence in areas of culture and conduct—in the censorship of books, the attacks on "immoral art," etc., and in the realm of private habits; yet it rarely was heard regarding the depredations of business or the corruption of politics. On this the churches were largely silent.

The moralizing temper had another consequence: the reinforcement of the "populist" character of American society. Long ago, travelers to these shores noticed the extreme egalitarianism of American manners and customs and warned of the "leveling" consequence of the glorification of the common, rather than the uncommon, man: for if one holds that each man is as good as the next, it is easy to say, as has often been the case, that no man can claim to be better than the next. Unfortunately, good and better are never defined. That no man should claim birth alone as the inherent possessor of a status is understandable; in that respect each man is as good as the next. But populism goes further: that some are more qualified than others to assert opinions is vehemently denied.

The populist imprint on American life has had its positive as well as negative sides. The idea of the "right of the people to know" is an underpinning of the guarantees of free press, of unrestrained inquiry, and of unhampered discussion. But in a populist setting, it operates without a sense of limits and often becomes an invasion of privacy. For what is it that "the people" have a right to know? One's morals and habits? One's political views? The earlier "reformers," self-appointed guardians of morals, insisted on the right of scrutiny of private conduct in the name of public decency. Later congressional investigators have insisted that the right to inquire is not bounded by legislative purpose but is an inherent aspect of the process of becoming the "public watchdog."

All these, in itself, would be less injurious to privacy—and freedom—if moralism and the populist conceptions of democracy were not also tied to a distinctive aspect of social control: the control of conduct, and the operation of sanctions against individuals through "public opinion" rather than law. Law, at least in the past, because it is tradition-bound and restrictive, is inhibitive of change and often has not squared with the experiences and needs of a people. But as the hard-won residue of human encounter with injustice, it sets up a strict set of procedures and a strict set of rules in admitting evidence and determining guilt. Americans, as an impatient people, however, have often been impatient with law, and the quicker sanctions of vigilantism and shaming through opinion have predominated. Moreover, the small-town character of much of the American temper derives its strength from the whispered play of gossip, from regulating conduct through public opinion rather than law. This was the exercise of conformity that was attacked so savagely by Sinclair Lewis in his *Main Street,* and the attack on the American small town was the leitmotif of the social criticism and literature of the twenties.

While in American culture the small town has been "defeated" (although in popular culture it has merged with the brassier tones of Hollywood), in American politics it has still held sway. A disproportionate percentage of the Congress, because of the gerrymandering of districts by rural-dominated legislatures, comes from small towns; these men usually have longer tenure and seniority, and the temper of the Congress, as an ideology, reflects the pseudo-egalitarian attitudes of the small town. So long as world-experiences could be assimilated into the perceptions of the small town, i.e., so long as one translated all problems into the small-town setting, the dichotomy of politics and moralism could prevail. Business was business, and church was church; and politics was a business. But with the growth of international ideologies, the breakdown of market mechanisms, the bewildering complexities of economic decisions, the rise of submerged groups, the anxieties of decision-making became overwhelming.

American political attitudes towards China and the defeat of Chiang Kai-shek is probably the clearest case in point. As Denis Brogan has pointed out, Americans, in their extraordinary optimism, find it hard to stand defeat; it is a sickening thrust at the omnipotence which, as an unconscious self-image, underlies American power. Hence, if Chiang Kai-shek's regime came toppling down, it

"Say, What Ever Happened To 'Freedom-From-Fear'?"

FIGURE 4. From *The Herblock Book* (Beacon Press, 1952).

was easier to ascribe the reason to betrayal—by the State Department or by intellectuals—than to recognize the complex reasons involving an understanding of the breakdown of Chinese institutions since the Republic of 1911, and the failure, because of civil war and invasion, to create a viable political structure in China.

The cry of betrayal and the charge of conspiracy is an old one in American politics. One of its chief roots is in the political Populist movement, which, in its grievances against the industrial order, found its devils among those who symbolized the monetary and credit system. Populism arose, after the Civil War, among the poor farmers of the South and West. It was a protest movement against the railroads, which by freely manipulating freight rates were able to "tax" the farmer unduly, and against the bankers, who by tightening money and credit and raising the interest rates made it difficult for the farmer to buy seed or pay off mortgages. While the grievances were real, and often legitimate, what the Populists could not perceive was that a system, and not individuals, was to blame. But politics is rarely won by attacking a system. The case of Tom Watson of Georgia is one in point. Watson, who ran for vice-president on the Populist ticket in 1896, was a pioneer muckraker whose "Watson's Jeffersonian Weekly" made pungent analyses of the system of tenant land tenure, of credit manipulation, and other evils in American life. But after the turn of the century, the Populist movement became fragmented, with large chunks of it following Bryan into the Democratic party, while other elements went over to the socialists. Watson became more rancorous. He attacked Wall Street, the international bankers, and finally the Jews. The identification of Jews with money power was an old one. Ignatius Donnelly, the spokesman for midwestern populism, had made this a central theme of his widely read novel *Caesar's Column* years earlier. Donnelly, however, had regarded the Jews as victims, since by virtue of medieval exclusions money-lending was one of the few trades open to them. Watson made the Jews the active agents of a closed conspiracy for world control. Watson was elected to the U.S. Senate, from Georgia, in 1920. He became the prototype of the new crop of Southern demagogues, Alabama's Tom Heflin, Mississippi's Theodore Bilbo, and Georgia's Eugene Talmadge. And yet, when he died, he could still be mourned by Eugene Debs as one who had fought for the people during his life.

In the twisted strands of populism one finds other, strange tales which on the surface seem metamorphoses, but which at bottom represent the workings out of the underlying Populist temper. William Lemke and Gerald Nye came out of the vigorous North Dakota Non-Partisan League, an independent grouping of radical farmers which, finding itself unable to operate outside the two-party system, had captured the Republican party of the state. North Dakota progressivism was one of the spearheads of reform and social legislation of the twenties and thirties; public power, anti-injunction laws, regulation of child labor, etc., etc. Nye led the famous investigation of the munitions-makers during the thirties which, to the sorrow of the historian, made the overly simple identification of the causes of war coterminous with the hunger for profits of the "merchants of death."

These men were "terrible simplifiers." All politics was a conspiracy, and at the center of the web were the "international bankers" and the "money changers." Thus, when war loomed in the late thirties, the suspicion of the bankers which was the root of the crabbed Populist mentality became focused on the Jews, and one found the strange spectacle of aging William Lemke running for president of the United States in 1940 on an open anti-Semitic ticket organized by Father Coughlin and his Social Justice Movement. (The vice-presidential candidate, it may be recalled, was Dr. Francis Townsend, whose old-age scheme featured a device to increase the circulation of money, while Father Coughlin, who became a national figure because of his radio sermons in the mid-thirties, had started out as a money reformer with the nickname of "Silver Charlie.") These simplifications, now somewhat attenuated, still formed a backdrop for more recent events. But other forces were at work, too.

An unsettled society is always an anxious one, and nowhere has this been truer than in the United States. In an egalitarian society, where status is not fixed, and people are not known or immediately recognizable by birth or dress, or speech or manners, the acquisition of status becomes all-important, and the threats to one's status anxiety-provoking. Gunnar Myrdal, in his investigation of the Negro problem in America, pointed out that class antagonisms are strongest between "adjacent" classes rather than the very bottom and the top. Thus, in the South, the deepest emotional resentment of the

Negro has come from the poor whites, and particularly from those once-poor whites who, having risen, sought more than ever to emphasize their distance from those below them. As one once was more royalist than the king, one becomes more traditionalist than even the settled families, and, in the case of nationality groups, more compulsively American than the older families.

The sociopsychological attitude that Myrdal discerned in the South has been equally characteristic of the immigrant pattern in American life. As each successive wave of people came over, they grouped together and viewed the next wave with hostility and fear. In the nineteenth century, the xenophobic strain was one of the deepest currents in American life. Before the Civil War, the Catholic was the chief target. There were riots, lynchings, and the burnings of convents in Boston in the 1820s. In 1832, the anti-Catholic movement was spurred by the publication of a book, *Foreign Conspiracy against the Liberties of the United States,* by Samuel F. B. Morse, who in the popular textbooks is accorded recognition only as a leading portrait painter and as the inventor of the telegraph. Fearing the spread of papal influence in Metternich's Europe, Morse formed the Anti-Popery Union to fight the Church. Out of its agitation grew a political party, the Native Americans, which sought to exclude all foreigners and to extend the naturalization period before citizenship to twenty years. The nativist sentiment elected James Harper mayor of New York in 1843 and was responsible, in part, for the election of Millard Fillmore as president in 1856. Anti-Catholic agitation was pushed into the background by the Civil War, but the tensions have remained to this day. In the East, Catholic political power came to the fore in the large urban cities of Boston, New York, Jersey City, and Chicago. In the Midwest it remained a political issue in the latter half of the nineteenth century through the agitation of the American Protective Association and the fundamentalist Protestant churches.

But what began as religious discrimination turned, in the decades that followed the Civil War, into social distinctions; these came when the rise of new social classes began to create status demarcations. In the expansion and prosperity of the 1870s and 1880s, Oscar Handlin points out:

Many a man having earned a fortune, even a modest one, thereafter found himself laboring under the burden of complex anxieties. He knew that success was by its nature evanescent. Fortunes were made only to be lost; what was earned in one generation would disappear in the next. Such a man, therefore, wished not only to retain that which he had gained; he was also eager for the social recognition that would permit him to enjoy his possessions; and he sought to extend these on in time through his family. . . . The last decades of the nineteenth century therefore witnessed a succession of attempts to set up areas of exclusiveness that would mark off the favored groups and protect them against excessive contact with outsiders. In imitation of the English model, there was an effort to create a "high society" with its own protocol and conventions, with suitable residences in suitable districts, with distinctive clubs and media of entertainment, all of which would mark off and preserve the wealth of the fortunate families.

This process of status demarcation, associated largely with wealth in the 1890s, in more recent years has been a problem for the rising ethnic groups which have sought recognition of their new position in American life. But the older means of such distinction have disappeared, because in the mass consumption economy all groups can easily acquire the outward badges of status and erase the visible demarcations. So it is largely through politics that the rising ethnic groups began to assert their new power and social position.

These elements of moralism, populism, Americanism, and status anxieties achieved a peculiar congruence in the fifties because of the changed nature of American politics: the emergence of foreign policy as the chief problem of politics. The politics of the 1930s were almost entirely domestic, and the sharp political conflicts of that decade were around economic issues, and the divisions in interest-group terms. The debate whether or not to go to war, although sharp, was extremely brief, and the war years were characterized by a high degree of national unity. But with the postwar emergence of Soviet Russia as the dominant force on the European continent, the breakup of the old colonial empires, the eruption of Communist challenges in China and Southeast Asia, and the war in Korea, the debate on the war from 1930–41 that was interrupted by Pearl Harbor was brought back, albeit in disguised form. The attempt to pin a charge of treason on the Democrats, the new nationalism of Bricker and Knowland, the reckless actions of McCarthy, represented, in extreme, aspects of that first debate. Thus the new issues no longer represented old interest-group or internal power divisions, but the playing-out of old frustrations and anxieties.

Few "symbols" are more representative of this change than the role of Dean Acheson. In the early days of the New Deal, Acheson, a young lawyer, resigned as assistant secretary of the treasury in protest against the "tinkering" with the dollar and the departure from orthodox practices; and Acheson was one of the symbols of conservative protest against the New Deal. A decade and a half later, as Truman's secretary of state, he had become the symbol of the "radical" policies of the Fair Deal. In those terms, of course, the conceptualization was meaningless.

But the fact that the arena of politics was now foreign policy allowed the moralistic strains to come to the fore. One of the unique aspects of American politics is that while domestic issues have been argued in hard-headed, practical terms, with a give-and-take compromise as the outcome, foreign policy has always been phrased in moralistic terms. Perhaps the very nature of our emergence as an independent country forced us to constantly adopt a moral posture in regard to the rest of the world; perhaps being distant from the real centers of interest conflict allowed us to employ pieties, rather than face realities. But since foreign policy has usually been within the frame of moral rather than pragmatic discourse, the debate in the fifties became centered in moral terms. And the singular fact about the Communist problem is that, on a scale rare in American political life, an ideological issue was equated with a moral issue and the attacks on communism were made with all the compulsive moral fervor which was possible because of the equation of communism with sin.

In itself this reflects a curious change in American life. While we gain a more relaxed attitude towards private morals, we are becoming rather more extremist in public life.

The "ideologizing" of politics gains reinforcement from another, independent tendency in American life, the emergence of what may be called the "symbolic groups." These are the inchoate entities known generally in capital letters as "Labor," "Business," the "Farmers," et al. The assumption is made that these entities have a coherent philosophy, a defined purpose, and that they represent tangible forces. This tendency derives from varied sources, but the biggest impetus has come from the changing nature of economic decision-making and the changing mode of opinion-formation in modern society. The fact that major economic decision-making has been centralized in the narrow cockpit of Washington, rather than spread over the impersonal market, leads groups like the National Association of Manufacturers, the Farm Bureau, the American Federation of Labor, etc., to speak for "Business," for "Labor," for the "Farmers." At the same time there is an increased sensitivity to "Public Opinion," heightened by the use of opinion polls in which the "Citizen" (not the specific individual with his specific interests) is asked what "Business" or "Labor" or the "Farmer" should do. In effect, these groups are often forced to assume a unique identity and a greater coherence beyond what they normally do.

Political debate, therefore, moves from specific clashes of interest, in which issues can be identified and possibly compromised, to ideologically tinged conflicts which polarize the various groups and divide the society.

The tendency to convert concrete issues into ideological problems, to invest them with moral color and high emotional charge, is to invite conflicts which can only damage a society. "A nation, divided irreconcilably on 'principle,' each party believing itself pure white and the other pitch black, cannot govern itself," wrote Walter Lippmann many years ago.

It has been one of the glories of the United States that politics has always been a pragmatic give-and-take rather than a series of wars-to-the-death. One ultimately comes to admire the "practical politics" of Theodore Roosevelt and his scorn for the intransigents, like Godkin and Villard, who, refusing to yield to expediency, could never put through their reforms. Politics, as Edmund Wilson has described T.R.'s attitude, "is a matter of adapting oneself to all sorts of people and situations, a game in which one may score but only by accepting the rules and recognizing one's opponents, rather than a moral crusade in which one's stainless standard must mow the enemy down."

Democratic politics means bargaining between legitimate groups and the search for consensus. This is so because the historic contribution of liberalism was to separate law from morality. The thought that the two should be separate often comes as a shock. In the older Catholic societies ruled by the doctrine of "two swords," the state was the secular arm of the church, and enforced in civil life the moral decrees of the church. This was possible in political theory, if not in practice, because the society was homogeneous, and everyone accepted the same religious values. But the religious wars that followed the Reformation proved that a plural society could only survive if it respected the principles of toleration. No group, be it Catholic or Protestant, could use the state to impose its moral conceptions on all the people. As the party of the *politiques* put it, the "civil society must not perish for conscience's sake."

These theoretical foundations of modern liberal society were completed by Kant, who, separating legality and morality, defined the former as the "rules of the game," so to speak; law dealt with procedural, not substantive, issues. The latter were primary matters of conscience, with which the state could not interfere.

This distinction has been at the root of the American democracy. For Madison, factions (or divergence of interests), being rooted in liberty, were inevitable, and the function of the Republic was to protect the causes of faction, i.e., liberty and the "diversity in the faculties of men," for "freemen, 'diverse' men, fallible, heterogeneous, heterodox, opinionated, quarrelsome man was the raw material of faction."

Since faction was inevitable, one could only deal with its effects, and not smother its causes. One way, of course, was, as adopted in the federal system, to separate the powers of government, so that no faction could easily secure a monopoly of power. But Madison knew that this was not enough. The threat to liberty would be reduced by representative government, and in this *extensive republic,* as he put it, the larger number of interests would "lessen the insecurity of private rights." But representative government, as John Stuart Mill cogently pointed out, must mean the representation of all interests, "since the interest of the excluded is always in danger of being overlooked." And being overlooked, as Calhoun added, constitutes a threat to civil order.

But representative government is important for the deeper reason that by including all representative interests one can keep alive "the antagonism of influences which is the only real security for continued progress." It is the only way of securing the "concurrent majorities," which, as Calhoun argued, was the solid basis for providing a check on the tyrannical "popular" majority. For only through representative government can one achieve consensus—and conciliation.

This is not to say that the Communist "interest" is a legitimate one, akin to the interest of other groups in the society, or that the Communist issue was completely irrelevant. As a conspiracy, rather than a legitimate dissenting group, the Communist movement remains a threat to democratic society. And by the criteria of "clear and present danger" democratic society may at times have to act against that conspiracy. But these are questions to be handled by law. The tendency to use the Communist issue as a political club against other parties or groups, or the tendency to convert questions of law into issues of morality (and thus shift the source of sanctions from the courts and legitimate authority to private individuals) can only create strains in a liberal society.

In the 170 years since its founding, American democracy has been rent only once by civil war. We have learnt since then, not without strain, to include the "excluded interests," the workers and the small farmers. These have secured a legitimate place in the American political equilibrium. And the ideological conflicts that almost threatened to disrupt the society, in the early years of the New Deal, have been mitigated.

The new divisions, created by the status anxieties of new middle-class groups, pose a new threat. The rancors of McCarthyism were one of its ugly excesses. However, the United States, so huge and complex that no single political boss or any single political group has ever been able to dominate it, will in time undoubtedly diminish these divisions, too. This is an open society, and these anxieties are part of the price we pay for that openness.

Talcott Parsons

McCARTHYISM AS SOCIAL STRAIN

Talcott Parsons, a professor of sociology at Harvard University, is a leading analytical sociologist and the author of The Structure of Social Action, The Social System, *and* Social Structure and Personality.

To the relatively objective observer, whether American or foreign, it seems clear that the complex phenomena that have come to be known as "McCarthyism" must be symptoms of a process in American society of some deep and general significance. Some interpret it simply as political reaction, even as a kind of neo-fascism. Some think of it as simply a manifestation of nationalism. The present paper proposes to bring to bear some theoretical perspectives of sociology in an attempt to work out an interpretation which goes beyond catchwords of this order.

McCarthyism can be understood as a relatively acute symptom of the strains which accompany a major change in the situation and structure of American society, a change which in this instance consists in the development of the attitudes and institutional machinery required to implement a greatly enhanced level of national political responsibility. The necessity for this development arises both from our own growth to an enormous potential of power, and from the changed relation to the rest of the world which this growth in itself, and other changes extraneous to American development, have entailed. The strains to which I refer derive primarily from conflicts between the demands imposed by the new situation and the inertia of those elements of our social structure which are most resistant to the necessary changes.

The situation I have in mind centers on the American position in international affairs. The main facts are familiar to all. It is not something that has come about suddenly, but the impact of its pressures has been cumulative.

The starting point is the relative geographical isolation of the

Talcott Parsons, "Social Strains in America—1955," in *The New American Right,* ed. Daniel Bell (New York, 1955). Copyright 1955 by S.G. Phillips, Inc. Reprinted by permission of the publisher.

United States in the "formative" period of its national history, down to, let us say, about the opening of the present century. The Spanish-American War extended our involvements into the Spanish-speaking areas of the Caribbean and to the Philippines, and the Boxer episode in China and our mediation of the Russo-Japanese War indicated rapidly growing interests in the Orient. Then the First World War brought us in as one of the major belligerents, with a brief possibility of taking a role of world leadership. From this advanced degree of international involvement, however, we recoiled with a violent reaction, repudiating the Treaty of Versailles and the League of Nations.

In the insuing period of "normalcy," until the shock of Pearl Harbor settled the question, it could still be held that the "quarrels" of foreign powers beyond the Americas were none of our concern, unless some "arbitrary" disturbance impinged too closely on our national interests. By the end of the Second World War, however, this attitude could not again be revived by any body of opinion which pretended to depend upon a realistic appraisal of our situation. Our own strength, in spite of our massive disarmament and demobilization, had grown too great; the defeat of France and the disorganization of Germany destroyed such continental European balance of power as had existed; Britain, though victorious, was greatly weakened in the face of worldwide commitments; and Soviet Russia emerged as a victorious and expanding power, leading with a revolutionary ideology a movement which could readily destroy such elements of stability favorable to our own national values and interests as still remained in the world. Along with all this have come developments in military technology that have drastically neutralized the protections formerly conferred by geographical distance, so that even the elementary military security of the United States cannot now be taken for granted apart from worldwide political order.

The vicissitudes of American foreign policy and its relations to domestic politics over this period show the disturbing effect of this developing situation on our society. We have twice intervened militarily on a grand scale. With a notable difference of degree, we have both times recoiled from the implications of our intervention. In the second case the recoil did not last long, since the beginnings of the cold war about 1947 made it clear that only American action was able to prevent Soviet domination of the whole continent of Europe. It can, however, be argued that this early and grand-scale resumption of responsibility imposed serious internal strains because it did not allow time for "digesting" the implications of our role in the war.

The outstanding characteristic of the society on which this greatly changed situation has impinged is that it had come to be the industrial society par excellence—partly because the settlement of the continental area coincided with the later industrial revolution, partly because of the immense area and natural resources of the country, but partly too because of certain important differences between American and European society. Since the United States did not have a class structure tightly integrated with a political organization that had developed its main forms before the industrial revolution, the economy has had a freedom to develop and to set the tone for the whole society in a way markedly different from any European country or Japan.

All highly industrialized societies exhibit many features in common which are independent of the particular historical paths by which their developments have taken place. These include the bureaucratic organization of the productive process itself, in the sense that the roles of individuals are of the occupational type and the organizations in which they are grouped are mainly "specific function" organizations. Under this arrangement the peasant type of agricultural holding, where farming is very closely bound up with a kinship unit, is minimized; so too of small family businesses; people tend to look to their productive function and to profit as a measure of success and hence of emancipation from conflicting ties and claims; the rights of property ownership are centered primarily in the organization which carries functional responsibility, and hence permits a high degree of segregation between private life and occupational roles for production purposes; contract plays a central part in the system of exchange, and para-economic elements tend to be reduced in importance.

Outside the sphere which touches the organization of the economy itself, industrialism means above all that the structures which would interfere with the free functioning of the economy, and of their adaptation to it, are minimized. The first of these is family and kinship. The American family system, chiefly characterized by the isolation of the nuclear or conjugal family, has gone farther than in any European society toward removing all interferences with the occupational roles of the breadwinning members, and with occupational mobility. A second field is religion. The American combination of federalism and the separation of church and state has resulted in a system of "denominational pluralism" which prevents organized religion from constituting a monolithic structure standing in the way of secular social developments. The third field concerns the matter of social stratification. The United States of course has a class structure; but it is one which has its primary roots in the system of occupational roles, and in contrast to the typical European situation it acts as no more than a brake on the processes of social mobility which are most important to an industrial type of occupational system. Under an effective family system there must be some continuity of class status from generation to generation, and there cannot be complete "equality of opportunity." In America, however, it is clearly the occupational system rather than kinship continuity that prevails.

Linked to this situation is our system of formal education. The United States was among the pioneers in developing publicly supported education; but this has taken place in a notably decentralized way. Not only is there no Department of Education in the federal government, but even the various state departments are to a large extent service organizations for the locally controlled school systems. Higher education further has been considerably more independent of class standards which equate the "scholar" with the "gentleman" (in a class sense) than has been the case in Europe. Also a far larger proportion of each age group attends institutions of higher education than in European countries.

Politically the most important fact about American industrialism is that it has developed overwhelmingly under the aegis of free enterprise. Historically the center of gravity of the integration of American society has not rested in the political field. There came to be established a kind of "burden of proof" expectation that responsibilities should not be undertaken by government unless, first, the necessity for their being undertaken at all was clearly established, and second, there was no other obviously adequate way to get the job done. It is therefore not surprising that the opening up of vast new fields of governmental responsibility should meet with considerable resistance and conflict.

The impact of this problem on our orientation to foreign relations has been complicated by an important set of internal circumstances. It is a commonplace that industrialism creates on a large scale two sets of problems which uniformly in all industrialized countries have required modifications of any doctrinaire "laissez faire" policy: the problems of controlling the processes of the economy itself, and of dealing with certain social repercussions of industrialization.

As the process of industrialization has developed in America there has been a steady increase in the amount of public control imposed on the economy, with the initiative mainly in the hands of the federal government. This trend was accelerated in the latter years of the nineteenth century, and has continued, with interruptions, through the New Deal. The New Deal, however, was more concerned with the social repercussions of industrialization, rather than with more narrowly economic problems. The introduction of a national system of social security and legislation more favorable to labor are perhaps the most typical developments. This internal process of government intervention has not gone far enough to satisfy European socialists, but it certainly constitutes a great modification of the earlier situation. Moreover, in broad lines it can be regarded as firmly established. It is significant that the major political parties now tend to vie with each other in promoting the extension of social security benefits, that there is no likelihood of repeal of the Federal Reserve Act, and that there is no strong movement to place the unions under really severe legal restraints.

On the whole, business groups have accepted the new situation and cooperated to make it work with considerably more good faith than in Continental Europe. Nevertheless, these internal changes have been sufficiently recent and far-reaching to keep the strains attendant on them from being fully resolved. Moreover they have created an important part of the problems with which this examination is chiefly concerned, problems touching the composition of the higher strata of the society, where the primary burden of responsibility must fall.

By contrast with European countries, perhaps in some ways particularly Britain, the United States has been conspicuous for the absence or relative weakness of two types of elite elements. The first of these is a hereditary upper class with a status continuous from preindustrial times, closely integrated with politics and public service. The second is an occupational elite whose roots are essentially independent of the business world—in the independent professions, the universities, the church, or government, including civil and military services.

In America the businessmen have tended to be the natural leaders of the general community. But, both for the reasons just reviewed and for certain others, this leadership has not remained undisputed. On the whole the business community has, step by step, resisted the processes of internal change necessitated by industrialization rather than taken the leadership in introducing them. The leadership that has emerged has been miscellaneous in social origin, including professional politicians, especially those in touch with the urban political machines, leaders in the labor union movement and elements in close touch with them. An important part has been played by men and women who may be said to exhibit a more or less "aristocratic" tinge, particularly in the Eastern cities, President Roosevelt of course having been among them. An important part has been played by lawyers who have made themselves more independent of the business connection than the typical corporation lawyer of a generation ago. Under the pressure of emergency, there has been a tendency for high military officers to play important roles in public life.

Another important group has been composed of "intellectuals"—again a rather miscellaneous assembly including writers, newspapermen, and members of university faculties. In general the importance of the university has been steadily enhanced by the increasingly technical character of the operations of the economy; businessmen themselves have had to be more highly educated than their predecessors, and have become increasingly dependent on still more highly trained technicians of various kinds.

The important point is that the "natural" tendency for a relatively unequivocal business leadership of the general community has been frustrated, and the business group has had to give way at many points. Nevertheless, a clearly defined nonbusiness component of the elite has not yet crystallized. In my opinion, the striking feature of the American elite is not what Soviet propaganda contends that it is—the clear-cut dominance by "capitalists"—but rather its fluid and relatively unstructured character. In particular, there is no clear determination of where political leadership, in the sense including both "politics" and "administration," is to center.

A further feature of the structure of American society is intimately related to the residual strains left by recent social changes. There is a continuing tendency for earlier economic developments to leave a "precipitate" of upper groups, the position of whose members is founded in the achievements of their ancestors, in this case relatively recent ones. By historical necessity these groups are strongest in the older parts of the country. Hence the cities of the Eastern seaboard have tended to develop groups that are the closest approach we have—though still very different from their European equivalent —to an aristocracy. They have generally originated in business interests, but have taken on a form somewhat similar to the mercantile aristocracies of some earlier European societies, such as the Hanseatic cities. In the perspective of popular democratic sentiments, these groups have tended to symbolize at the same time capitalistic interests and social snobbery. In certain circumstances they may be identified with "bohemianism" and related phenomena which are sources of uneasiness to traditional morality.

As the American social and economic center has shifted westward, such groups in the great Middle Western area and beyond have been progressively less prominent. There the elites have consisted of new men. In the nature of the case the proportional contribution to the economy and the society in general from the older and the newer parts of the country has shifted, with the newer progressively increasing their share. But at the same time there is the sense among them of having had to fight for this share against the "dominance" of the East. A similar feeling permeates the lower levels of the class structure. A major theme of the Populist type of agrarian and other radicalism had combined class and sectional elements, locating the source of people's troubles in the bankers and railway magnates of the East and in Wall Street. It must not be forgotten that the isolationism of the between-the-wars period was intimately connected with this sectional and class sentiment. The elder La Follette, who was one of the principal destroyers of the League of Nations, was not a "conservative" or in any usual sense a reactionary, but a principal leader of the popular revolt against "the interests."

It must also not be forgotten that a large proportion of the American population are descendants of relatively recent immigrants whose cultural origins are different from the dominant Protestant

Anglo-Saxon elements. A generation and more ago the bulk of the new immigration constituted an urban proletariat largely dominated by the political machines of the great cities. By now a great change has taken place. The children of these immigrants have been very much Americanized, but to a considerable degree they are still sensitive about their full acceptance. This sensitivity is if anything heightened by the fact that on the whole most of these elements have risen rapidly in the economic and social scale. They are no longer the inhabitants of the scandalous slums; many have climbed to lower-middle-class status and higher. They have a certain susceptibility to "democratic" appeals which are directed against the alleged snobbery of the older dominant elements.

Finally, the effect of the great depression of the 1930s on the leading business groups must not be forgotten. Such a collapse of the economy could not fail to be felt as a major failure of the expectation that business leaders should bear the major responsibility for the welfare of the economy as a whole and thus of the community. In general it was not the businessmen but the government, under leadership which was broadly antagonistic to business, which came to the rescue. Similarly, the other great class of American proprietors, the farmers, had to accept governmental help of a sort that entailed controls, which in turn inevitably entailed severe conflicts with the individualistic traditions of their history. The fact that the strains of the war and postwar periods have been piled so immediately on those of depression has much to do with the severity of the tensions with which this analysis is concerned.

My thesis, then, is that the strains of the international situation have impinged on a society undergoing important internal changes which have themselves been sources of strain, with the effect of superimposing one kind of strain on another. What responses to this compound strain are to be expected?

It is a generalization well established in social science that neither individuals nor societies can undergo major structural changes without the likelihood of producing a considerable element of "irrational" behavior. There will tend to be conspicuous distortions of the patterns of value and of the normal beliefs about the facts of situations. These distorted beliefs and promptings to irrational action will also tend to be heavily weighted with emotion, to be "overdetermined" as the psychologists say.

The psychology of such reactions is complex, but for present purposes it will suffice to distinguish two main components. On the negative side, there will tend to be high levels of anxiety and aggression, focused on what rightly or wrongly are felt to be the sources of strain and difficulty. On the positive side there will tend to be wishful patterns of belief with a strong "regressive" flavor, whose chief function is to wish away the disturbing situation and establish a situation in phantasy where "everything will be all right," preferably as it was before the disturbing situation came about. Very generally then the psychological formula tends to prescribe a set of beliefs that certain specific, symbolic agencies are responsible for the present state of distress; they have "arbitrarily" upset a satisfactory state of affairs. If only they could be eliminated the trouble would disappear and a satisfactory state restored. The role of this type of mechanism in primitive magic is quite well known.

In a normal process of learning in the individual, or of developmental change in the social system, such irrational phenomena are temporary, and tend to subside as capacity to deal with the new situation grows. This may be more or less easily achieved of course, and resolution of the conflicts and strains may fail to be achieved for a long period or may even be permanently unsuccessful. But under favorable circumstances these reactions are superseded by an increasingly realistic facing of the situation by institutionalized means.

Our present problem therefore centers on the need to mobilize American society to cope with a dangerous and threatening situation which is also intrinsically difficult. It can clearly only be coped with at the governmental level; and hence the problem is in essence a matter of political action, involving both questions of leadership— of who, promoting what policies, shall take the primary responsibility—and of the commitment of the many heterogeneous elements of our population to the national interest.

Consequently there has come to be an enormous increase in pressure to subordinate private interests to the public interest, and this in a society where the presumptions have been more strongly in favor of the private interest than in most. Readiness to make commitments to a collective interest is the focus of what we ordinarily mean by "loyalty." It seems to me that the problem of loyalty at its core is a genuine and realistic one; but attitudes toward it shade all the way from a reasonable concern with getting the necessary degree of loyal cooperation by legitimate appeals, to a grossly irrational set of anxieties about the prevalence of disloyalty, and a readiness to vent the accompanying aggression on innocent scapegoats.

Underlying the concern for loyalty in general, and explaining a good deal of the reaction to it, is the ambivalence of our approach to the situation: The people in the most "exposed" positions are on the one hand pulled by patriotic motives toward fulfillment of the expectations inherent in the new situation; they want to "do their bit." But at the same time their established attitudes and orientations resist fulfillment of the obligation consequence for the resistance to be displaced or projected on to other objects which function as scapegoats. In the present situation it is precisely those parts of our population where individualistic traditions are strongest that are placed under the greatest strain, and that produce the severest resistances to accepting the obligations of our situation. Such resistances, however, conflict with equally strong patriotic motives. In such a situation, when one's own resistance to loyal acceptance of unpalatable obligations, such as paying high taxes, are particularly strong, it is easy to impute disloyal intentions to others.

Our present emotional preoccupation with the problem of loyalty indicates above all that the crisis is not, as some tend to think, primarily concerned with fundamental values, but rather with their implementation. It is true that certain features of the pattern of reaction, such as tendencies to aggressive nationalism and to abdication of responsibilities, would, if carried through, lead to severe conflict with our values. But the main problem is not concerned with doubts about whether the stable political order of a free world is a goal worth sacrificing for, but rather with the question of how our population is rising or failing to rise to the challenge.

The primary symbol that connects the objective external problem and its dangers with the internal strain and its structure is "Communism." "World Communism" and its spread constitute the features of the world situation on which the difficulty of our international problem clearly centers. Internally it is felt that Communists and their "sympathizers" constitute the primary focus of actual or potential disloyalty.

With respect to the external situation, the focus of the difficulty in the current role of Soviet Russia is of course reasonable enough. Problems then arise mainly in connection with certain elements of "obsessiveness" in the way in which the situation is approached, manifested for instance in a tendency to subordinate all other approaches to the situation exclusively to the military, and in the extreme violence of reaction in some circles to the Chinese situation, in contrast to the relative tolerance with which Yugoslavia is regarded.

Internally, the realistic difficulty resides mainly in the fact that there has indeed been a considerable amount of Communist infiltration in the United States, particularly in the 1930s. It is true that the Communist party itself has never achieved great electoral success, but for a time Communist influence was paramount in a number of important labor unions, and a considerable number of the associations Americans so like to join were revealed to be Communist-front organizations, with effective Communist control behind the public participation of many non-Communists. Perhaps most important was the fact that considerable numbers of the intellectuals became fellow-travelers. In the days of the rise of Nazism and of the popular front, many of them felt that only Soviet Russia was sincere in its commitment to collective security; that there was a Franco-British "plot" to get Germany and Russia embroiled with each other, etc. The shock of the Nazi-Soviet pact woke up many fellow-travelers, but by no means all; and the cause was considerably retrieved by Hitler's attack on Russia.

Two other features of the Communist movement which make it an ideal negative symbol in the context of the present loyalty problem are the combination of conspiratorial methods and foreign control with the progressive component of its ideological system. On the one hand the party has drastically repudiated the procedures of constitutional democracy, and on this issue has broken with all the democratic socialist parties of Europe; it claims the protection of democratic procedures and civil liberties, but does not hesitate to abuse them when this seems to be advantageous. There has further never been any question of the American party determining its own policies by democratic procedures. Perhaps in fact the knowledge of the extent to which the "front" organizations have been manipulated from behind the scenes has been the most disillusioning aspect for liberal Americans of their experience with communism at home.

At the same time the movement had a large content of professed idealism, which may be taken to account for the appeal of communism before the cold war era for such large elements of liberal opinion in the United States, as in other Western countries. Marx was, after all, himself a child of the Enlightenment, and the Communist movement has incorporated in its ideology many of the doctrines of human rights that have formed a part of our general inheritance. However grossly the symbols of democracy, of the rights of men, of peace and brotherhood, have been abused by the Communists, they are powerful symbols in our own tradition, and their appeal is understandable.

Hence the symbol "Communism" is one to which a special order of ambivalence readily attaches. It has powerful sources of appeal to the liberal tradition, but those who are out of sympathy with the main tradition of American liberalism can find a powerful target for their objections in the totalitarian tactics of communism and can readily stigmatize it as "un-American." Then, by extending their objections to the liberal component of Communist ideology, they can attack liberalism in general, on the grounds that association with Communist totalitarianism makes anything liberal suspect.

These considerations account for the anti-Communist's readiness to carry over a stereotype from those who have really been party members or advanced fellow-travelers to large elements of the intellectuals, the labor movement, etc., who have been essentially democratic liberals of various shades of opinion. Since by and large the Democratic party has more of this liberalism than has the Republican, it is not surprising that a tendency to label it as "sympathizing" with or "soft toward" communism has appeared. Such a label has also been extended, though not very seriously, to the Protestant clergy.

But there is one further extension of the association that is not accounted for in these terms, nor is failure to include certain plausible targets so accountable. The extension I have in mind is that which leads to the inclusion as "pro-Communist" of certain men or institutions that have been associated with political responsibility in the international field. Two symbols stand out here. The first is Dean Acheson. Mr. Acheson has for years served the Democratic party. But he has belonged to the conservative, not the New Deal wing of the party. Furthermore, the coupling of General Marshall with him, though only in connection with China, and only by extremists, clearly precludes political radicalism as the primary objection, since Marshall has never in any way been identified with New Deal views. The other case is that of Harvard University as an alleged "hotbed" of communism and fellow-traveling. The relevant point is that Mr. Acheson typifies the "aristocrat" in public service; he came of a wealthy family, he went to a select private school (Groton) and to Yale and Harvard Law School. He represents symbolically those Eastern vested interests, against whom antagonism has existed among the new men of the Middle West and the Populist movement, including the descendants of recent immigrants. Similarly, among American universities Harvard has been particularly identified as educating a social elite, the members of which are thought of as "just the type," in their striped trousers and morning coats, to sell out the country to the social snobs of European capitals. It is the combination of aristocratic associations—through the Boston Brahmins—and a kind of urban-bohemian sophistication along with its devotion to intellectual and cultural values, including precisely its high intellectual standards, which makes Harvard a vulnerable symbol in this context.

The symbol "Communism," then, from its area of legitimate application, tends to be generalized to include groups in the population who have been associated with political liberalism of many shades and with intellectual values in general and to include the Eastern upper-class groups who have tended to be relatively internationalist in their outlook.

A second underlying ambivalent attitude-structure is discernible in addition to that concerning the relation between the totalitarian and the progressive aspects of communism. On the one hand, communism very obviously symbolizes what is anathema to the individualistic tradition of a business economy—the feared attempt to destroy private enterprise and with it the great tradition of individual freedom. But on the other hand, in order to rise to the challenge of the current political situation, it is necessary for the older balance between a free economy and the power of government to be considerably shifted in favor of the latter. We must have a stronger government than we have traditionally been accustomed to, and we must come to trust it more fully. It has had in recent times to assume very substantial regulatory functions in relation to the economy, and now vastly enhanced responsibilities in relation to international affairs.

But, on the basis of a philosophy which, in a very different way from our individualistic tradition, gives primacy to "economic interests," namely the Marxist philosophy, the Communist movement asserts the unqualified, the totalitarian supremacy of government over the economy. It is precisely an actual change in our own system in what in one sense is clearly this direction that emerges as the primary focus of the frustrations to which the older American system has been subjected. The leaders of the economy, the businessmen, have been forced to accept far more "interference" from government with what they have considered "their affairs" than they have liked. And now they must, like everyone else, pay unprecedentedly high taxes to support an enormous military establishment, and give the government in other respects unprecedentedly great powers over the population. The result of this situation is an ambivalence of attitude that on the one hand demands a stringent display of loyalty going to lengths far beyond our tradition of individual liberty, and on the other hand is ready to blame elements which by ordinary logic have little or nothing to do with communism, for working in league with the Communist movement to create this horrible situation.

Generally speaking, the indefensible aspect of this tendency in a realistic assessment appears in a readiness to question the loyalty of all those who have assumed responsibility for leadership in meeting the exigencies of the new situation. These include many who have helped to solve the internal problems of the control of the economy, those who in the uneasy later thirties and the first phase of the war tried to get American policy and public opinion to face the dangers of the international situation, and those who since the war have tried to take responsibility in relation to the difficult post . . . who are also presumptively tainted with communism. Here again, admittedly, certain features of our historical record and attitudes provide some realistic basis for this tendency. In fact many elements in both parties have failed lamentably to assess correctly the dangers of the situation, both internally and externally. New Dealers have stigmatized even the most responsible elements of the business world as economic royalists and the like, while many elements in business have clung long past a reasonable time to an outmoded belief in the possibility of a society with only a "night watchman" government. In foreign affairs, some members of the Democratic party have been slow to learn how formidable a danger was presented by totalitarian communism, but this is matched by the utopianism of many Republicans about the consequences of American withdrawal from international responsibilities, through high tariffs as well as political isolationism. The necessity to learn the hard realities of a complex world and the difficulty of the process is not a task to be imposed on only part of the body politic. No party or group can claim a monopoly either of patriotic motive or of competent understanding of affairs.

In a double sense, then, communism symbolizes "the intruder." Externally the world Communist movement is the obvious source of the most serious difficulties we have to face. On the other hand, although communism has constituted to some degree a realistic internal danger, it has above all come to symbolize those factors that have disturbed the beneficent natural state of an American society which allegedly and in phantasy existed before the urgent problems of control of the economy and greatly enhanced responsibility in international affairs had to be tackled.

Against this background it can perhaps be made clear why the description of McCarthyism as simply a political reactionary movement is inadequate. In the first place, it is clearly not simply a cloak for the "vested interests" but rather a movement that profoundly splits the previously dominant groups. This is evident in the split, particularly conspicuous since about 1952, within the Republican party. An important part of the business elite, especially in the Middle West and in Texas, the "newest" area of all, have tended in varying degrees to be attracted by the McCarthy appeal. But other important groups, notably in the East, have shied away from it and apparently have come to be more and more consolidated against it. Very broadly, these can be identified with the business element among the Eisenhower Republicans.

But at the same time the McCarthy following is by no means confined to the vested-interest groups. There has been an important popular following of very miscellaneous composition. It has comprised an important part of those who aspire to full status in the American system but have, realistically or not, felt discriminated against in various ways, especially the midwestern lower and lower middle classes and much of the population of recent immigration origin. The elements of continuity between western agrarian populism and McCarthyism are not by any means purely fortuitous. At the levels of both leadership and popular following, the division of American political opinion over this issue *cuts clean across the traditional lines of distinction between "conservatives" and "progressives,"* especially where that tends to be defined, as it so often is, in terms of the capitalistic or moneyed interests as against those who seek to bring them under more stringent control. McCarthyism is *both* a movement supported by certain vested-interest elements *and* a popular revolt against the upper classes.

Another striking characteristic of McCarthyism is that it is highly selective in the liberal causes it attacks. Apart from the issue of communism in the labor unions, now largely solved, there has been no concerted attack on the general position of the labor movement. Further, the social program aimed toward the reduction of racial discrimination has continued to be pressed, to which fact the decision of the Supreme Court outlawing segregation in public education and its calm reception provide dramatic evidence. Nevertheless, so far as I am aware there has been no outcry from McCarthyite quarters to the effect that this decision is further evidence of Communist influence in high circles—in spite of the fact that eight out of nine members of the present Court were appointed by Roosevelt and Truman.

Perhaps even more notable is the fact that, unlike the 1930s, when Father Coughlin and others were preaching a vicious anti-Semitism, anti-Semitism as a public issue has since the war been very nearly absent from the American scene. This is of course associated with full employment. But particularly in view of the rather large and conspicuous participation of Jewish intellectuals in the fellow-traveling of the 1930s, it is notable that Jewishness has not been singled out as a symbolic focus for the questioning of loyalty. A critical difference from German Nazism is evident here. To the Nazis the Jew was the *primary* negative symbol, the Communist the most prominent secondary one. But it must also be remembered that capitalism was symbolically involved. One of the functions of the Jew was to *link* communism and capitalism together. This trio were the "intruders" to the Nazis. They symbolized different aspects of the disturbance created by the rapid development of industrialism to the older preindustrial *Gemeinschaft* of German political romanticism. It was the obverse of the American case—a new economy destroying an old political system, not new political responsibilities interfering with the accustomed ways of economic life.

Negatively, then, the use of the symbol "Communism" as the focus of anxiety and aggression is associated with a high order of selectivity among possibly vulnerable targets. This selectivity is, I submit, consistent with the hypothesis that the focus of the strain expressed by McCarthyism lies in the area of political responsibility —not, as Marxists would hold, in the structure of the economy as such, nor in the class structure in any simple, Marxian-tinged sense.

The same interpretation is confirmed by the evidence on the positive side. The broadest formula for what the McCarthyites positively "want"—besides the elimination of all Communist influence, real or alleged—is perhaps "isolationism." The dominant note is, I think, the regressive one. It is the wishful preservation of an old order, which allegedly need never have been disturbed but for the wilful interference of malevolent elements, Communists and their sympathizers. The nationalistic overtones center on a phantasy of a happy "American way" where everything used to be all right. Naturally it is tinged with the ideology of traditional "laissez faire," but not perhaps unduly so. Also it tends to spill over into a kind of irritated activism. On the one hand we want to keep out of trouble; but on the other hand, having identified an enemy, we want to smash him forthwith. The connection between the two can be seen, for example, in relation to China, where the phantasy seems to be that by drastic action it would be possible to "clean up" the Chinese situation quickly and then our troubles would be over.

The main contention of these pages has been that McCarthyism is best understood as a symptom of the strains attendant on a deep-seated process of change in our society, rather than as a "movement" presenting a policy or set of values for the American people to act on. Its content is overwhelmingly negative, not positive. It advocates "getting rid" of undesirable influences, and has amazingly little to say about what should be done.

This negativism is primarily the expression of fear, secondarily of anger, the aggression which is a product of frustration. The solution, which is both realistically feasible and within the great American tradition, is to regain our national self-confidence and to take active steps to cope with the situation with which we are faced.

On the popular level the crisis is primarily a crisis of confidence. We are baffled and anxious, and tend to seek relief in hunting scapegoats. We must improve our understanding and come to realize our strength and trust in it. But this cannot be done simply by wishing it to be done. I have consistently argued that the changed situation in which we are placed demands a far-reaching change in the structure of our society. It demands policies, and confidence, but it demands more than these. It demands above all three things. The first is a revision of our conception of citizenship to encourage the ordinary man to accept greater responsibility. The second is the development of the necessary implementing machinery. Third is national political leadership, not only in the sense of individual candidates for office or appointment, but in the sense of social strata where a traditional political responsibility is ingrained.

The most important of these requirements is the third. Under American conditions, a politically leading stratum must be made up of a combination of business and nonbusiness elements. The role of the economy in American society and of the business element in it is such that political leadership without prominent business participation is doomed to ineffectiveness and to the perpetuation of dangerous internal conflict. It is not possible to lead the American people *against* the leaders of the business world. But at the same time, so varied now are the national elements which make a legitimate claim to be represented, the business element cannot monopolize or dominate political leadership and responsibility. Broadly, I think, a political elite in the two main aspects of "politicians" whose specialties consist in the management of public opinion, and of "administrators" in both civil and military services, must be greatly strengthened. It is here that the practical consequences of McCarthyism run most directly counter to the realistic needs of the time. But along with such a specifically political elite there must also be close alliance with other, predominantly "cultural" elements, notably perhaps in the universities, but also in the churches.

In the final sense, then, the solution of the problem of McCarthyism lies in the successful accomplishment of the social changes to which we are called by our position in the world and by our own domestic requirements. We have already made notable progress toward this objective; the current flareup of stress in the form of McCarthyism can be taken simply as evidence that the process is not complete.

Political Critiques

Nelson W. Polsby
McCARTHYISM AT THE GRASS ROOTS

Nelson W. Polsby, formerly of the political science faculties at the University of Wisconsin, and Wesleyan University, is a member of the political science faculty at the University of California at Berkeley, and the author of Community Power and Political Theory.

The recent appearance of an apparently definitive journalistic post-mortem on Senator Joseph McCarthy underscores the rather striking professional inattention of political scientists to one of the most spectacular political phenomena of our time. For those of us who view political science as a potentially powerful weapon in the cause of rational political decision-making, this lost opportunity seems especially poignant. If it is too late to assist politicians in determining the extent to which they should have allowed themselves to be imprisoned by the demands and the rhetoric of McCarthy and his followers, it is not too late to ask more academic questions about who McCarthy's followers really were, and about the sources and extent of his power.

Three Hypotheses

This paper is by no means the first attempt to discuss the social sources and political pretensions of McCarthyism. In fact, numerous ingenious explanations of the McCarthy phenomenon have been proffered. Furthermore, sophisticated students have seldom relied upon any single explanation. In reducing previous explanations to three hypotheses, then, I have no doubt greatly simplified the viewpoints of the writers who first suggested them.

One hypothesis which attempts to account for McCarthy's rise to prominence lays heavy stress on "atmospheric" conditions surround-

Nelson W. Polsby, "Toward an Explanation of McCarthyism," *Political Studies* (October 1960): 250–264. Reprinted by permission of the Clarendon Press, Oxford.

ing the position of the United States after the Second World War.
Instead of being allowed to relax into their customary interwar posture of "normalcy," Americans were faced with the necessity of
continuing their foreign entanglements, owing to the hostility of the
Russians and the debilitation of our overseas allies. This hypothesis
suggests that many Americans were unhappy at this turn of events,
and that many of them interpreted these events as the inexorable
result of involvement in "foreign" wars. These citizens opposed
large-scale spending for foreign economic aid, were progressively
angered by the fall of China and the discovery of atomic spies both
here and abroad, had always been sceptical of alliances with Great
Britain, and became bitterly frustrated at the seemingly endless
maneuvers of the cold war and the Korean conflict. Senator Mc-
Carthy's approach to politics, so runs the argument, gave support
to the nostalgia of isolationists, many of whom had ancestral ties
with Germany, and was congenial to those who harboured populistic
and anglophobic sentiments.

From this hypothesis we should deduce that McCarthy would find
support among people of German extraction, among isolationists,
and among those who preferred dramatic activity to patience in the
conduct of foreign affairs. Evidence on these points is not conclu-
sive, but certainly suggests the plausibility of this hypothetical description of McCarthy supporters. For example, Samuel Lubell has
reported two chief sources of strength for Senator McCarthy:

> *One was the frustrations that arose out of the Korean War, which often
> took the form of voters demanding "Why don't we clean up these Com-
> mies at home with our boys dying in Korea?" . . . The second main source
> of McCarthy strength came in areas which opposed our entry into the
> last war.*

Lubell also indicates that McCarthy ran better in those Wisconsin
townships with high German populations than he did in the rest of
the state.

Hodges, Graham, and Anderson, in a study of Pierce County,
Wisconsin, discovered that McCarthy supporters could be found disproportionately among those of German extraction, and among those
who are "sceptical about foreign involvements on the part of the
United States . . . [favoring] discontinuing both economic and mili-

tary aid to Asiatic and European nations, and [feeling] that the Korean conflict was a mistake."

Information from various Gallup surveys is also relevant. A study of New London County, Connecticut, indicated that one of the major reasons people gave for supporting McCarthy was that "They admire greatly his 'courage' and 'sincerity,' feeling that he is not afraid to 'get tough.' " Gallup also reported a similar response among citizens of East Stroudsburg, Pennsylvania, where many citizens favored McCarthy because of his "fearlessness," and because he "gets a lot done the way he goes about things."

It seems likely that the political atmosphere contributed in some general sense to McCarthy's rise, and supplied his followers with rationalizations for supporting him. But presumably this atmosphere existed for everyone, and, save in the case of the relatively small German-American group, the hypothesis does not explain, for the purpose of assessing his political possibilities at any time, where in the population most of McCarthy's supporters could have been located.

Many people have been persuaded that McCarthy's potential was considerable, since for a great length of time Gallup surveys recorded that a substantial proportion of the population "approved of" McCarthy in some sense. The atmospheric hypothesis differentiates only crudely between those favorable to McCarthy and those unfavorable, on the basis of generalized attitudes towards historical events, and identifies more exactly only a small portion of McCarthy's alleged followers.

A second hypothesis derives from the researches of Adorno and his associates and identifies McCarthy as an authoritarian leader. Authoritarianism implies a host of rather misanthropic social attitudes including "toughness," superconformity, intolerance, generalized hostility, and an unusual concern with sexual "goings on." Many observers, pointing out that Senator McCarthy exhibited more than his share of these hostile attitudes, deduced that throughout the population those individuals who were most authoritarian would be most likely to be McCarthyites.

This hypothesis has gained some confirmation, but contrary evidence suggests the need for more precise specification of the personality characteristics which are supposed to have caused pro-McCarthy sentiments.

Hodges, Graham, and Anderson report that McCarthyites were "more conformistic, agreeing that there are too many 'odd-balls' around, that the 'good' American doesn't stand out among his fellow Americans, and that children should not develop hobbies which are . . . unusual"; and more misanthropic, "concurring with statements that 'people are out to cheat you,' and that 'there is wickedness, cheating and corruption all about us.' "

However, some students have noticed that there were relatively intolerant groups in the population whose members nevertheless seemed markedly impervious to McCarthy's charismatic charm. And, conversely, it has been established that members of other groups which were not notably intolerant have supported him to a disproportionate degree. A third hypothesis attempts to account for these findings by making reference to the needs and aspirations of certain groups within the population which were satisfied, it is suggested, through McCarthyite activity.

The authors of *The New American Right* have advanced this hypothesis in its most full-blown and persuasive form. This volume is a collection of essays by a distinguished group of social scientists, all attempting to explain the social sources and consequences of McCarthyism. The nature of American politics has changed, they say, so as to render the McCarthy movement unintelligible to conventional forms of political analysis. They call for a "new" type of analysis, one that recognizes the significance of the emergence of status groups as entities making important demands upon the rest of American society, through the political system. In times of economic distress demands are made along class lines; economic "interests" divide the nation's wealth and income by putting pressures of various kinds upon one another and on the government, which acts as a mediating and legitimizing agent for society and as a forum for the expression of dissatisfactions and the promulgation of panaceas. In periods of prosperity the continuing adjustments of interests to each other and to the resources of the economy yield the center of political attention to the demands of status groups, which use the arena to insist on the improvement or maintenance of their status position in society. In times of economic well-being the "dynamic of dissent" resides in those status groups who wish to change the status quo— and of course consider themselves at a disadvantage in the status hierarchy. The McCarthy movement, the authors agree, expresses a noneconomic form of protest which can only mean that those in society who supported McCarthy did so because of status dissatisfactions.

The authors could have predicted from this hypothesis those groups which should be pro-McCarthy and those which should be anti-McCarthy. Secondly, they could have checked these predictions against the available evidence. In fact, they took only one of these steps, deducing who McCarthy's followers might be. It can easily be seen from an inspection of Table 1 that the "status politics" hypothesis is much too inclusive to have very much explanatory power. Although it may accurately estimate why specific members of each of the groups named may have found McCarthy an attractive political figure (i.e., because of their status anxieties) it neither differentiates successfully among groups, nor provides criteria by which some groups can be excluded from its purview.

A second step would have been to check deductions against facts. Only Lipset, among *The New American Right* essayists, attempted to do so, and he presents only his conclusions from findings, rather than the findings themselves. At the time of publication of *The New American Right* there were several sources available which might have confirmed at least partially some of the predic-

TABLE 1
Groups Comprising the New American Right
(i.e., McCarthyites)

I. *Named in six out of seven essays:* New rich.

II. *Named in five essays:* Texans, Irish, Germans.

III. *Named in four essays:* Middle class, Catholics, Midwesterners.

IV. *Named in three essays:* Lower middle class, up-mobile, less educated.

V. *Named in two essays:* "Cankered intellectuals," old family Protestant "shabby genteel," recent immigrants, down-mobile, minority ethnics, Old Guard GOP, ex-Communists, Midwest isolationists.

VI. *Named in one essay:* Lower class, small town lawyers, auto dealers, oil wildcatters, real estate manipulators, small business men, manual workers, elderly and retired, rentier class, youth, Southern Californians, South Bostonians, fringe urbanites in middlesized cities, transplants to city, Polish Catholics, hick Protestants, patriotic and historical group members (e.g. DAR), Scandinavians, Southern Protestant fundamentalists, soured patricians, small town residents, neo-fascists.

Source: Daniel Bell, ed., *The New American Right* (New York, 1955).

TABLE 2
Groups Comprising the New American Right,
According to Empirical Evidence

The vertical axis ranks groups according to the number of essays out of seven in which they are explicitly mentioned in *The New American Right.* The horizontal axis lists sources of empirical data in support of (Yes) or against (No) the listing of groups as nuclei of New American Right sentiment.

Group	Gallup	Bean	Harris
5			
(1) Germans	—	No	—
(2) Irish	—	—	No
4			
(3) Catholics	Yes	Yes	—
3			
(4) Less educated	Yes	Yes	
2			
(5) Minority ethnics	Yes & No	Yes & No	Yes & No
(6) Republicans	Yes	—	—
(7) Recent immigrants	Yes & No	Yes & No	—
1			
(8) Lower class	Yes	Yes	—
(9) Manual workers	Yes	—	—
(10) Polish Catholics	—	Yes	—
(11) Elderly	Yes	—	—
(12) Youth	No	—	No
(13) Scandinavians	—	No	—
Groups not named in *The New American Right*			
(1) Farmers	Yes	Yes	—
(2) New Englanders	Yes	—	—

Sources: American Institute of Public Opinion (Gallup Poll), *Influences in the Mid-Term Election,* 1954 (Bean), *Is There A Republican Majority?* (Harris).

tions made in these essays. I present the relevant conclusions of these sources in Table 2.

As Table 2 indicates, the 'status anxieties' hypothesis yields rather indifferent results, since it apparently fails to account for two groups in the populace found to have been disproportionately pro-McCarthy, yet on the other hand evidence indicates that some groups named as McCarthyite in fact were not. Although there is no reason to be enthusiastic about the quality of the sources on which these conclusions are based, they are very much better than mere surmises about McCarthy's grass roots followers. Given the speculative nature of most writing on McCarthy, attention should be paid to these empirical findings, despite their limitations.

Other criticisms can be made of *The New American Right.* The assertion that "status groups" are at the heart of the McCarthy movement is essentially trivial. The task was to determine *which* status groups were peculiarly situated so as to be especially favorable to McCarthy. And the identification of some of the groups named as McCarthyite is simply implausible. This should weigh heavily in the case of the book under discussion, where the basic argument depends on plausibility rather than more "scientific" demonstrations of truth. For example, it is unclear why members of the DAR should release status anxieties by joining in an attack on the very social groups whose history their organization celebrates. That status anxieties can drive people to attack others—especially the weak—is a reasonable enough argument, but if it is in principle possible to negate *The New American Right* thesis in any way, surely the cases of white Protestant "shabby genteel" McCarthyites succeed in doing so. Finally, it should be noted that the introduction of ethnic and status considerations into political analysis can hardly be said to have originated with the authors of *The New American Right,* as they themselves, aware of the practices of "ticket balancing," the folklore of political "availability," and long-standing academic interest in the group conflict theory of politics, no doubt realize.

Since the publication of *The New American Right,* Martin Trow has come forward with new data bearing on the "status anxieties" hypothesis. He concludes from his study of Bennington, Vermont, that: (1) supporters of McCarthy were not more politically intolerant than nonsupporters of McCarthy when formal education was held constant. McCarthy received a disproportionate share of his support from the less educated members of the community, who are always less tolerant. (2) McCarthy received much greater support from those members of the middle class who were *economically* at a disadvantage (e.g., small business men) and who expressed hostility toward modern forms of political and economic organization.

These findings support all three hypotheses in so far as they

identify McCarthyites as members of a movement of generalized protest. But they also indicate that economic and political factors may
have been as important as status anxieties in explaining the social
sources of McCarthyism.

A Political Interpretation

I want to turn now to a fourth hypothesis, one which attempts to
explain McCarthyism as a political phenomenon. It is a surprising
fact that analysts have discounted so heavily the purely political
aspect of his success. Therefore I want to review now the rather
heavy evidence supporting the hypothesis that McCarthy succeeded
at the grass roots primarily among Republicans.

TABLE 3
Popularity of Senator Joseph McCarthy

In general, would you say you have a favorable or unfavorable
opinion of Senator Joseph R. McCarthy?

	N	%
Favorable	456	31
Unfavorable	693	46
No opinion	287	19
Don't know him	41	3
	1,477	99

Source: Gallup Survey 529 K, 6 April 1954.

TABLE 4
**Sentiment about Germany of Those Favorable and Unfavorable
to Senator J. McCarthy**

Would you, yourself, like to see Germany again become one of
the three or four most powerful countries?

	F (%)	U (%)
Yes	29	25
No	56	59
No opinion	7	8
Qualified	8	8
	100	100
	(N = 454)	(N = 690)

Source: Gallup Survey 529 K, April 1954.

TABLE 5

Political Information of Those Favorable and Unfavorable to Senator J. McCarthy

Will you please tell me which of these men you have heard of? And will you tell me what country he is from?

	Favorable			Unfavorable		
	Chiang (%)	Mao (%)	Nehru (%)	Chiang (%)	Mao (%)	Nehru (%)
Yes, correct country	89	34	60	88	42	67
Yes, incorrect or don't know country	6	19	12	8	20	9
Not heard of, no answer	5	47	28	4	38	24
	100	100	100	100	100	100
	(N = 458)	(N = 455)	(N = 454)	(N = 700*)	(N = 689)	(N = 690)

Source: Gallup Survey 529 K, April 1954.
* The fact that the Ns here exceed the total unfavorable population of 693 is perhaps on account of double responses in a small number of cases.

For example, I present . . . in Table 3 the results of a reanalysis of a Gallup survey. In this reanalysis I have attempted to differentiate between those who were for and those against McCarthy. Pro- and anti-McCarthy populations were selected by tabulating responses to the following question: "In general, would you say you have a favorable or unfavorable opinion of Senator Joseph McCarthy?"

The data at hand were limited; none the less they provided an opportunity to test in some approximate way the predictions of each of the hypotheses thus far offered to account for McCarthy's grass roots support.

The nationwide questionnaire tapped possible pro-German sentiments among respondents, with the results shown in Table 4. The results, while not extreme, are in the direction indicated by the "atmospheric" hypothesis.

Authoritarians, it is said, tend to be politically confused and badly informed. The nationwide survey asked a series of questions designed to elicit political information of various kinds. McCarthyites and non-McCarthyites were able to identify Far Eastern political leaders correctly to about the same degree, but, once again, the slight differences recorded were all in the expected direction. This

TABLE 6
Political Participation of Those Favorable and Unfavorable to Senator J. McCarthy

Question I. Have you ever voted in any election, or don't you pay any attention to politics?
Question II. In the election in November 1952, did things come up which kept you from voting, or did you happen to vote?

| | Favorable | | Unfavorable | |
	I (%)	II (%)	I (%)	II (%)
Yes	86	77	89	81
No	3	20	2	14
Never	11	—	9	—
No, too young	—	3	—	5
	100	100	100	100
	(N = 456)	(N = 455)	(N = 692)	(N = 687)

Source: Gallup Survey 529 K, April 1954.

.TABLE 7

Religious Preference of Those Favorable and Unfavorable to Senator J. McCarthy

Question: What is your religious preference—
Protestant, Catholic, or Jewish?

	F (%)	U (%)
Protestant	68	71
Catholic	28	20
Jewish	1	5
Other	2	3
	99	99
	(N = 452)	(N = 685)

Source: Gallup Survey 529 K, April 1954.

is also true of the questions asking about participation in the last election, and in elections generally (see Tables 5, 6).

The same thing happens when crude tests of the 'status' hypothesis are applied, the assumption being that a higher proportion of McCarthyites come from the Catholic, lower class, and less educated parts of the population. Table 7 shows, once again, tendencies in the direction of confirmation.

* * *

But this relatively meager empirical confirmation is unimpressive when set against comparable figures describing the two populations by their political affiliations. . . .

These findings speak for themselves, but do not stand alone. The distributions of McCarthy's vote in Wisconsin, where, it should be admitted, "The impact [of McCarthyism] on the political and cultural life of the state was not particularly great," indicate strongly that McCarthy ran best in the most heavily Republican areas, and conversely. James G. March has demonstrated this point conclusively with respect to the 1952 primary election. Samuel Lubell has observed that Senator McCarthy in 1952 ran well ahead of his state average in townships populated heavily by people of German extraction, but this also was true of other Republicans, including Senator

Taft in the 1952 primary, and Republican Presidential candidates in 1944, 1948, and 1952. Inspection of election returns bears out the thesis that McCarthy ran best where the Republican party was strongest. McCarthy's strongest showing in 1952, for example, generally took place in those counties giving Walter Kohler, Republican candidate for governor, their heaviest support. Out of the seventy-one counties in Wisconsin, thirty gave McCarthy a margin of 2 to 1 or better, and of these thirty, twenty-four were counties in which Governor Kohler beat his opponent by 3 to 1 or more. In the twenty-nine counties where he made his strongest race, capturing 75 percent or more of the two-party vote, Kohler received only 28 percent, of his statewide vote. But in the thirty counties where McCarthy received 65 percent of the vote or more, fully 35 percent of McCarthy's statewide vote was concentrated.

These figures demonstrate that the McCarthy vote was concentrated in areas of Republican strength, and was neither scattered, nor distributed in some pattern unique to McCarthy, nor particularly strong.

Deciding where McCarthyites at the grass roots were located is of course not sufficient to explain his success in official Washington. Many cogent reasons for McCarthy's success have been given, and since they are mutually complementary it is unnecessary to choose between them. McCarthy was, at first, the weapon of a desperate Republican party. Senator Taft's famous advice, "If one case doesn't work, then bring up another," is a measure of the lengths to which Republicans were willing to go in those days to embarrass a long-entrenched Democratic administration. Secondly, there was McCarthy's protected position as a member of the Senate. While he was never even remotely a significant member of the Club, attacks on him might have been construed by powerful Senators as attacks on Senatorial prerogatives and practices. McCarthy's place in the Senate also gave him the protection of immunity from libel suits, the services of the staff of a committee, and the powers to hold hearings and issue subpoenas.

Third, one can scarcely discount his personal effectiveness as an imaginative political entrepreneur who exploited the mass media by accommodating his "exposés" to the exigencies of deadlines, and who employed the bulging briefcase, the nonexistent "document," garbled figures, and so on, with stunning effect. A fourth reason for

McCarthy's success was no doubt the vulnerability (real or imagined) of the Truman administration on the issue of Communists in government, and a fifth reason would certainly be the emasculation of administrative resistance to McCarthy's activities, by order of President Eisenhower.

V McCARTHYISM: TWO CONCLUSIONS

Harold Lord Varney

McCARTHY: AS THE VOICE OF THE PEOPLE

Harold Lord Varney was an articulate contributor to the debate over McCarthy in the opinion journals in 1954. An agile literary controversialist, he was one of the few of Senator McCarthy's advocates who argued for the senator on the basis of what were thought to be his accomplishments as well as the delinquencies of his critics.

The loudly ballyhooed left wing drive that was going to blast Joe Mc-Carthy out of the United States Senate is showing signs of collapse.

The mud guns are still erupting but it's not McCarthy, it's the smearers who are now in trouble. Senator Lehman, Walter Reuther, Edward R. Murrow, and a few more diehards are still popping off, but such furious challengers of yesterday as ex-Senator Tydings, ex-Senator Benton, ex-Congresswoman Douglas and the fading Drew Pearson aren't talking much any more about McCarthy. Despite frantic efforts of the *Daily Worker* and the *Reporter* to keep the smear train going, the steam has gone out of the boilers.

Back in February 1950, when McCarthy made his famous Wheeling speech disclosing the Communist putrefaction in the State Department, few would have given odds on his survival. The Truman-ADA-Communist forces arrayed against him seemed too overwhelming.

But today—four years and some billions of words of smear copy later—the silencing of Joe McCarthy doesn't look so easy. The great accuser has revealed a political indestructibility which has amazed his haters. Two recent incidents accent the fact.

On June 1, 1950, at the worst moment of the Acheson-Tydings counterattack on McCarthy, seven Senate Republicans, believing that they were playing good politics, issued a "Declaration of Conscience" repudiating the Wisconsin Senator. It was generally believed at the time that this thrust from his own camp would finish Joe off. It didn't.

What happened to the seven Republicans? One died. Another left the party. But of the remaining five, not a single one voted

Harold Lord Varney, "What Has Joe McCarthy Accomplished?" *American Mercury* (May 1954): 3–14. Reprinted by permission of the *American Mercury.*

against McCarthy on February 2, 1954, when he came before the
Senate for an increased appropriation for his Subcommittee on Investigations. McCarthy got his appropriation by a Senate vote of
85 to 1. The "conscience" Republicans had made a singular recovery
from their qualms.

Another straw was even more revealing. Early last January the
Gallup Poll sampled national opinion on McCarthy. This was a
follow-up of several previous pollings. Gallup found that, after ab-
sorbing the most venomous smear attack of our times, McCarthy in
1954 stands at the all-time peak of his national support.

Fifty percent of those sampled by the poll were favorable to the
senator against only 29 percent unfavorable. As late as August 1953,
the count had stood at 34 percent favorable; 42 percent unfavorable.

The meaning of this extraordinary public opinion shift is unmistakable. Despite all the dead cats, it is McCarthy who has voiced the
actual mood of the American people during the last four years. It is
his left-minded challengers and their dupes, mostly concentrated in
Washington and New York, who have been out of tune.

When we search for the keys to McCarthy's extraordinary political
achievement, we are struck first by the ironic role which the senator's enemies have played in his build-up. Walter Reuther, in his
recent speech before the Canadian editors, shed bitter tears over
the contribution of the newspapers to McCarthy's present stature.
The point which Reuther missed was that the press placed the Wisconsin Senator on page one only after his maligners, including
Reuther himself, had unleashed a slander campaign against him of
almost unparalleled venom.

But even more important than the disrepute of his adversaries in
building his prestige has been his impressive record of result-getting.
The senator has not batted one hundred on his many inquiries of the
last four years, but his score of success has been so high as to
amaze even the skeptical. In anti-McCarthy propaganda, a stock
argument has been the denial that he has actually accomplished
anything important. The facts speak convincingly for McCarthy.

For purposes of review it must be recalled that the McCarthy inquiries fall into two separate periods. The first, from February 1950
to January 1953 saw him a minority member of the Senate (often not
wholeheartedly aided by his fellow Republicans) without official
power of subpoena or investigation.

The second period commenced in January 1953 when McCarthy became chairman of the Senate Committee on Government Operations, with an annual fund of $200,000 (later increased to $214,000) to conduct inquiries. During this current period, he has enjoyed the power of subpoena, and has been able effectually to follow through his inquiries. Obviously a different yardstick must be used for the two periods.

Without attempting to recapitulate all of McCarthy's antisubversive activities in the pre-1953 period, a few citations will indicate their scope. His first task was to break down the encrusted smugness and assurance of the Acheson ring in the State Department. When we remember the cocky arrogance and insolence of Dean Acheson and his favorites during the period of the China White Paper of July 30, 1949, and the Acheson and Truman "hands off" statements of January 1950, we can envisage the difficulty of such a task.

Only a slashing frontal attack would have availed. Striking for the jugular, the senator in his famous Senate speech of February 20, 1950, produced a list of eighty-one State Department employees, past or present, who were serious security risks—citing them at first by number instead of name, in fairness to those who could prove innocence.

The validity of the McCarthy charges is shown by the fact that virtually every individual on this February 20, 1950, list is now out of the State Department, either by resignation or dismissal.

Subsequently, McCarthy named several other even more important State Department figures as serious security risks, including Owen Lattimore, Ambassador Philip C. Jessup, John Carter Vincent, Haldore Hanson, John Stewart Service, Oliver Edmund Clubb and Edward K. Posniak. At the announcement of each of these names, the abuse and invective rose to storm heat. McCarthy was striking now at key figures in the Acheson ring, and every weapon of coercion and intimidation was invoked, including the threat of expulsion from the Senate. But McCarthy didn't scare.

After the name-calling had run its course, McCarthy's boxscore on these State Department principals stood as follows:

1. Owen Lattimore, dropped from the directorship of the Walter Hines Page School at Johns Hopkins, and indicted by the Federal Grand Jury for perjury.

2. Philip C. Jessup, refused a favorable vote for confirmation by the Senate Foreign Affairs Committee in 1952, when President Truman reappointed him ambassador to the United Nations, and retired unconfirmed.

3. John Carter Vincent, permitted to retire from the State Department on March 4, 1953, on the ground that his performance of duty had fallen short of the standards required "at this critical time."

4. Haldore Hanson, taken out of a sensitive executive post in the Point Four division and transferred to minor work.

5. John Stewart Service, dismissed from the State Department on December 13, 1951, on the ground that there was "reasonable doubt" of his loyalty.

6. Oliver Edmund Clubb, declared a security risk by the State Department Loyalty Board in February 1952 but permitted to retire on pension by Acheson.

7. Edward G. Posniak, permitted to resign after the McCarthy exposure.

The important thing to note, in these major exposés, is that each one was cited at first by the senator's scoffers as another instance of McCarthy shotgun accusation. In the end, even a Truman State Department found it necessary in every case to backtrack and accept the McCarthy conclusions.

Thanks to the McCarthy fight, the Acheson coterie went out of the State Department on January 3, 1953, a dazed and discredited band. It had taken just three years to reverse the whole Washington atmosphere.

Having demonstrated what he could accomplish as a free lance, McCarthy in January 1953 when he became chairman of the Government Operations Committee, stepped into a new role. In an administration distinguished by a score or more of simultaneous congressional investigations into Truman misrule, it is McCarthy's committee which has held the spotlight. It has done so by sheer force of steady, driving attack.

The surprising thing, to those who had unquestioningly believed the smear stories, was the scrupulous fairness of a McCarthy investigation. The nation saw only the full-dress public hearings, at which individuals with a strong presumption of guilt were examined. What it did not see was the long and painstaking pattern of preliminary investigation which preceded these spectacular occasions. In the preliminaries, hundreds of reputed security risks were examined, with no publicity and no injury to reputation. The innocent were winnowed out. Only hardened "Fifth Amendment" cases, or individuals of clear guilt or unfitness were subjected to the pitiless light of the public session. In these sessions, McCarthy was frankly tough. He had to be tough in order to break down the brazen defiance and the bureaucratic insolence of most of his examinees.

Statistics are disembodied things, but it is enlightening to know that during the first session of the 83rd Congress, the McCarthy committee initiated 157 separate investigations. It conducted 445 preliminary inquiries which did not lead to further investigations. It examined 546 witnesses in public or private sessions, and turned up 79 Fifth Amendment Communists. Most of these inquiries were pointed at situations which had long been festering but which no one, before McCarthy, had seriously scrutinized.

The most spectacular McCarthy job, in the first session, was the probe of the Voice of America.

Prior to this inquiry, the VOA had enjoyed a status as a sort of sacred cow among government agencies. Set up initially by William Benton, while he was assistant secretary of state, its personnel was waterlogged with left-minded and incompetent men who owed their jobs to "connections" in high Truman circles.

When McCarthy looked into the Voice, he found such miscast individuals as Reed Harris, W. Bradley Connors, Edwin M. J. Kretzman, Dr. William Johnstone, Jr., Theodore Kaghan and Raymond Gram Swing conducting this supposedly anti-Communist propaganda operation.

With scant cooperation from his own Republican administration, and with ribald abuse from the liberal left, McCarthy broke the grip of the holdovers on the VOA. American-minded staff members, long cowed by their superiors, came boldly before the committee and drew a picture of waste and mismanagement which couldn't be shrugged off. Harris, Kaghan, Swing, Connors and Johnstone were soon on their way out.

McCarthy himself would be the first to concede that the VOA job is finished. Theodore C. Streibert, Eisenhower appointee as director of the USIE, which supervises the Voice, has made the self-revealing statement that we are not fighting international communism: we are fighting Russian imperialism. A Voice, guided by such an extraordinary concept of America's propaganda task, would be a weak instrument against the advance of communism.

A parallel condition of top incompetence was found in the VOA engineering department, whose chief engineer, it was discovered, had never even attended an engineering school. Committee inquiries uncovered staggering waste in the so-called Baker West and Baker East transmitter construction jobs. By halting these ill-planned projects, the committee saved the American taxpayer at least $18 million.

But the move which really infuriated the left-of-center brethren was the McCarthy inquiry into the libraries. The whole public discussion of the library issue has been conducted in a smoke screen of high-level lying and distortion.

What was at stake was, of course, the question whether pro-Communist printed matter should be bought and displayed overseas by the International Information Administration as approved American propaganda. The issue was distorted by McCarthy's enemies into one of "book burning" and thought suppression.

The United States, as a part of its propaganda against communism, maintains 285 library centers in Europe, Asia, Africa, and South America. These libraries are widely used by intellectuals in all countries. Only a fool or a pro-Communist would suggest that pro-Russian or pro-Chinese Communist publications be included in a book list designed to sell America. And yet Senator McCarthy's committee discovered that 30,000 of the 2,000,000 volumes in these libraries had been authored by Communist or pro-Communist writers. Books by Earl Browder, William Z. Foster, Howard Fast, Mrs. Paul Robeson, James S. Allen, Gene Weltfish, Herbert Aptheker, Morris U. Schappes, Corliss Lamont and numerous other Sovietolators had been bought by the USIS for these exhibit libraries of Americanism.

The entrance of the McCarthy committee into the library situation was the signal for a frantic attempt at window-dressing by the USIS. During the succeeding four months, no less than ten directives on book purchases were issued by the State Department, each compounding the existing confusion. Finally, on July 9, a permanent policy was enunciated which met some of the McCarthy objections.

Before this happened, however, the American Library Association, primarily through the politicking of Luther H. Evans, former Librarian of Congress and New Deal careerist, kicked up a terrific

"You Read Books, Eh?"

FIGURE 5. From *The Herblock Book* (Beacon Press, 1952).

rumpus, charging that McCarthy, in trying to exclude Communist books from USIS libraries, was engaging in "book burning" and thought suppression. It was an asinine demonstration to come from the nation's top librarians, but for a time it seemed likely to snowball when President Eisenhower, in a speech at Dartmouth College, made an impromptu attack on "book burning." The left-wingers were deliriously happy: this is the beginning of the break between Ike and McCarthy, they exulted.

But their rejoicing was short-lived. President Eisenhower made a public statement declaring that he had not been referring to McCarthy in his "book burner" sentence. The senator, as usual, came out of the library controversy with added stature.

Another 1953 McCarthy task which showed the senator in a constructive light was his investigation of the violations of the China embargo (technically a licensing system) by our supposed allies. A task force of the committee, headed by Robert F. Kennedy, made a searching study of the present Western trade with Red China. It discovered that since December 1951 there had been a sharp increase in this malodorous commerce. It found that of the 162 Western-flag vessels involved in the China trade, as of April 20, 1953, 100 were British. They were being protected in China waters by the British Navy.

When the committee looked into this subject, it was appalled to discover that the State Department, despite the Battle Act barring United States assistance to nations shipping war materials to our enemies, was not clear in its mind concerning actual American policy. At a hearing on May 4, 1953, John M. Leddy, acting deputy assistant secretary of state for economic affairs, told Senator McCarthy, under questioning, that "we are not now seeking at this time the discontinuance of all trade and all shipping to Red China." Such a shocking admission stirred the senator to a determination to do something about it.

An opportunity presented itself in the case of the Greek-owned vessels. These tramp ships, operating under different flags (63 of them under the British flag), were carrying 35 percent of the illicit China trade. The directing headquarters of this Greek vessel trade is in New York. Members of the committee staff contacted the Greek owners and secured their pledge to withdraw all their ships from the China trade, for the duration of the Korea state of war. This meant the removal from China commerce of 327 vessels, with a total tonnage of 3.5 million tons. The Greek owners pointed out to the committee that no American official had ever previously asked them to remove their vessels from this Communist trade.

Such imaginative action by McCarthy in this and similar situations has contributed to his growing Washington legend.

His surprise probe of the security system at the General Printing Office found the senator back in his original quest for Communists in the government. Because confidential official documents pass through the GPO for printing, it is an exposed leak point in our security set-up. Unfortunately, information reached the committee that the GPO security system was dangerously lax.

Moving energetically into the GPO situation, the committee examined S. Preston Hipsley, GPO director of personnel. The Hipsley testimony was eye-opening. When asked if it was the policy of the GPO loyalty board not to discharge an employee merely for membership in the Communist party, Hipsley replied, "That is true." He went on to explain that this policy had been laid down for the respective loyalty boards by Seth W. Richardson, Federal Loyalty Board chairman under the Truman-Acheson regime. Speaking of Richardson, Hipsley told the senator, "He was our guide."

The prize exhibit in the GPO probe was Edward Rothschild, who was found working in the assembly room up to the date of the investigation, with access to top secret documents. Rothschild had been identified to the FBI by forty separate witnesses as a Communist party member. He had been under investigation by the GPO loyalty board for more than three years but, although all the FBI data was available to them, the board members had done nothing. A quick result of the McCarthy hearings was the discharge of Rothschild, and the replacement of the lax loyalty board.

In August 1953 after considerable previous research, Senator McCarthy turned his scrutiny upon one of the most potentially dangerous Communist trouble spots in the United States—the laboratories of the Army Signal Corps, particularly Fort Monmouth in Eatontown, New Jersey. In these laboratories, Army and civilian scientists are working on one of the most hush-hush projects in the defense establishment—the development of radar protection against possible air raids.

What centered attention on Fort Monmouth was the fact that

Julius Rosenberg, executed Communist atom spy, and Joel Barr, his associate, had worked at Fort Monmouth during the war, and had reputedly set up a Communist cell there. The FBI and Army Intelligence had kept the personnel at Fort Monmouth under close observation, to determine whether any part of the cell was still in existence. McCarthy had little expectation that his inquiries would turn up an actual Red spy at this late date. What he hoped to accomplish in Fort Monmouth was to determine how the pattern of Communist infiltration had developed in the radar laboratories, to spotlight the potential danger points in the personnel, and, importantly, to discover whether there was any laxity in Army administration of security protection.

A total of 194 witnesses were heard by the committee, 35 of them in public sessions. No Rosenbergs were discovered, but several extremely dubious staff members were brought to light. The frightening fact about the inquiry was that in the public hearings 20 witnesses connected with the radar program invoked the Fifth Amendment when questioned about Communist and, in some cases, espionage activities.

The most disquieting discovery of the inquiry was the presence in Fort Monmouth, in a high administrative position, of Aaron H. Coleman, schoolmate and friend of Julius Rosenberg, who had been inducted by Rosenberg, according to testimony given, into the Young Communist League. Records showed that Coleman had also been listed by Morton Sobell, convicted Rosenberg spy ring member, as an employment reference. As late as January 1952 Coleman had been the $9,600-a-year chief of the systems section at the Evans Signal Laboratory at Fort Monmouth.

What disturbed McCarthy was the fact that as long ago as September 1946 Army investigators had found forty-eight classified documents in Coleman's home, which he had removed from the laboratory. So lax was the security system that Coleman, after a ten-day suspension, was restored to his job and later promoted. Again in 1951, the FBI had sent a lengthy and urgent report on Coleman to Fort Monmouth only to have it ignored.

The Fort Monmouth inquiry is still in progress, with many open ends. So far, the findings convincingly justify the stress which the senator has placed upon the project.

McCarthy's questioning mind has led him increasingly into the subject of the Army. Like most Americans, he has been concerned over the multiplying signs that a deadly dangerous condition of dry rot has attacked some of the branches of the military establishment. The recurrent scandals in Army procurement and construction show that, while most of the officer corps is sound, the Army has its black sheep and its plain incompetents.

McCarthy found himself drawn into Army investigation by the indications of unsuspected Communist infiltration at control points. One aspect of the Army which drew his concern was the indoctrination material which was being put in the hands of officers and noncoms. Incredible as it may seem, there were distinct evidences that Communist and pro-Soviet writers had succeeded in winning acceptance as authors or contributors to these indoctrination booklets. What disturbed McCarthy was the fact that high officers of the Army, charged with supervision over this program, were so ill-informed about communism that they were unaware of what was happening.

Inquiry revealed that the Army was using Sir Bernard Pares' *A History of Russia* as a basic indoctrination course textbook. Sir Bernard was identified by Louis F. Budenz, ex-Communist leader, as a secret member of the British Communist party.

The appalling thing about the committee investigation was its revelation of the abysmal ignorance of General Richard C. Partridge, then head of the Army's G-2, and in charge of the indoctrination work. Questioned by Roy M. Cohn about his knowledge of elementary Communist terms, General Partridge flunked every question. When pinned down, he admitted he had read only two books on Russia, but could not recall the author of one of them. And yet a man so ill-informed was at a choke point where he passed upon all the indoctrinational work of the Army.

His Army inquiries eventually brought Senator McCarthy into sharp and dramatic conflict with Secretary of the Army Stevens. McCarthy, in his years as investigator, had learned that in dealing with top bureaucrats, both Army and civilian, only a vigorous and aggressive questioning will elicit the facts. Stevens, reflecting the controlling clique at the Pentagon, objected to McCarthy's driving questioning of Brigadier General Ralph W. Zwicker, commander of Camp Kilmer, in the case of the alleged cover-up of Major Irving Peress.

Records available as early as April 1953 showed that Peress was a member of the Communist party, and had taken a false oath in declaring that he was not, in obtaining his commission. And yet in November 1953 with this evidence in the files, the Army gave Peress a promotion. When subpoenaed by the McCarthy committee, Peress confirmed the supposition of his communism by pleading the Fifth Amendment. Shortly thereafter he asked for a discharge—a step which would have given him an escape from any further Army discipline. Suspecting that Peress might try this trick, the senator wrote to the Pentagon asking that Peress be held in the Army pending the preparation of court martial charges. To McCarthy's consternation, he learned that on February 2, the day following the receipt of his letter at the Pentagon, General Zwicker at Camp Kilmer had signed honorable discharge papers for Peress.

Outraged at this exhibition of Army softness, McCarthy called Zwicker before the committee. It was immediately apparent that the general intended to give the committee little if any cooperation. Under the senator's questioning, the general put on a disgraceful exhibition of evasion and doubletalk. He revealed that he had signed the honorable discharge papers under instructions from the Pentagon. But the name of the Pentagon dunderhead who had thus deliberately covered up for a proven Communist was stubbornly refused.

Secretary of the Army Stevens here made an incredible blunder. Instead of ordering Zwicker to give the withheld information to the committee, Stevens intervened to back up Zwicker. He worsened the situation by forbidding other officers to appear before McCarthy for questioning. Overnight, Stevens became the hero of all the left wing national press. For a time it seemed that an ugly head-on encounter between Stevens and McCarthy was imminent.

But the secretary, recognizing the shakiness of his position, hastily retreated from his stand just on the eve of a personal appearance before the committee, and he issued an order that officers should honor McCarthy's subpoena. Throughout the whole incident, President Eisenhower was under extreme pressure from the McCarthy-haters in his immediate entourage to leap into the controversy and rebuke McCarthy. The president allowed seven days to pass after Stevens' capitulation before he talked. Then, at his press conference, he read an 800-word prepared statement which fell so far short of the denunciation of McCarthy which had been expected that it stunned the whole tribe of smearers. It did not mention McCarthy by name.

This whole Stevens incident was probably McCarthy's greatest Washington victory. It established the fact of his formidable personal power, based upon a prodigious national following, beyond cavil or denial.

Other inquiries have come under the restless supervision of McCarthy during his first year of chairmanship. These have included (1) a full-dress study of the personnel filing system of the State Department with a view to correcting the loyalty record confusion which the senator had encountered during the secretaryship of Acheson; (2) an investigation of the part played by Harry D. White and V. Frank Coe in the transfer to Soviet Russia of U.S. occupation currency plates in the period immediately following the war; (3) a study of the horrifying facts in regard to Communist atrocities against American soldiers in the Korean War; (4) an inquiry looking toward the betterment of the auditing system covering grants to the states, particularly in connection with the Social Security program; (5) a study of the stockpiling of strategic materials; (6) an investigation of the presence of a Hiss defense contributor in the CIA.

Any attempt, such as we have made, to profile a public figure in the full morning of his career must suffer from the flaw of evanescence. While we are still assessing his past, McCarthy is likely to be galloping away on new quests and new kleig-lighted conflicts.

Like him or not, it is generally acknowledged that Joe McCarthy is the most controversial figure that American politics has thrown up since FDR. His ill-wishers have watched him with keyhole intentness to catch him in a slip, but he has brilliantly baffled them. His admirers are a growing and dedicated company.

Within the Republican party, McCarthy's position is strategic. After Eisenhower, he looms as the only Republican who commands a great following among the Democrats. The most startling fact brought out in the January Gallup Poll was that McCarthy is approved by almost a majority of the sampled Democrats. McCarthy has continuously exasperated the Eisenhower leaders (the president's brother, Arthur, on July 24 of last year indicated how the family probably actually feels about him), but the president and his counselors know that it would be suicidal to affront the senator's vast following.

All newspaper chatter about a clash between the president and McCarthy may be dismissed as idle surmise. The great conservative core of the Republican party—leaderless since the death of Senator Taft—would be an uncertain quantity in such a contest.

McCarthy is where he is today because he satisfies the deep national hunger for an affirmative man. In a Washington of vacillating, irresolute, pressure-group-cowed politicians, he stands out in sharp relief as a man sure of himself. His unshaken, self-confidence is shown by the opponents whom he has tackled: they have been Marshall, Acheson, Tydings, Conant—men in the full tide of their authority. And he has never lost a major Washington fight.

McCarthy, although he has made mistakes, has never made the ineffable mistake of wearying the people. He sometimes gets too far out in front of public opinion, but so far public opinion has always followed him. Even when he irritates, he amuses. Even when he is repetitious, he repeats in a different style.

Because he takes the long-shot chances that other men avoid, he cannot help but endear himself to an American public which cherishes sportsmanship. Because he is a fighter who continuously faces and enjoys the fire of the whole liberal left, he appeals to the unfailing American instinct for the underdog.

His enemies desperately scan the political horizon for an issue that will stop him, but the probability is that he has climbed too high now to be headed. His current clashes with the Pentagon are a serious hazard. The higher Army incompetents are an entrenched and vengeful company. But in communism, McCarthy has an issue of such tremendous voltage that it will be difficult for his baiters to focus national attention on anything else during the years just ahead.

As Russia and Red China advance nightmarishly toward the maximum power goals which they will reach in the nineteen seventies, the American people will be as unlikely to think seriously of anything else, as to ignore an onrushing comet. Communism will be *the* issue of the fifties and the sixties. Those American leaders who most surely interpret the emotions of the American public in the face of the Communist challenge will be the men who will dominate American politics.

Today, Senator McCarthy is the articulate voice of the American people in a Communist-haunted age. On this issue, he marches with history. He cannot lose.

Richard Rovere

McCARTHY: AS NATIONAL DEMAGOGUE

Richard Rovere is a free-lance writer, author of the "Washington News-letter" in the New Yorker, *co-author of* The General and the President, *and author of* Howe and Hummel, Their True and Scandalous History.

Senator Joe McCarthy (R., Wis.) died ten years ago, on May 2, 1957, of causes never fully explained, though evidently connected with an ailment of the liver. While not the work of his own hand or that of any other man, his death has been called suicide by some, murder by others. Those who say suicide maintain that he allowed and even encouraged life to slip away, that he deliberately chose not to do what his doctors insisted that he do in order to live. Those who say murder mostly agree with the late George Sokolsky, who wrote: "He was hounded to death by those who could not forget and would not forgive." There is probably a bit of truth in both contentions.

He was forty-eight when he died. However, his career as perhaps the most gifted and successful demagogue this country has ever known had to come to an end two and a half years earlier, when on December 2, 1954, the Senate voted, 67 to 22, to censure him for various offenses committed against the presumed dignity of the institution and the self-esteem of its members. And that vote took place less than five years after he had broken out of obscurity by waving before an audience in Wheeling, West Virginia, a piece of paper that he said was a "list" of Communists "working and making policy" in the State Department and "known to the Secretary of State" to be conscious agents of the Soviet Union. Before that day—February 9, 1950—he was unknown outside Washington and Wisconsin and not very well known in either the capital or the state whose voters had absent-mindedly sent him to the Senate and were, he had reason to believe, getting ready to retire him in 1952. But a few months after the Wheeling speech he was known throughout the country and around the world, and he was a great power in American politics. He was probably the first American ever to be

From Richard H. Rovere, "The Most Gifted and Successful Demagogue This Country Has Ever Known," *New York Times Magazine*, April 30, 1967. © 1967 by the New York Times Company. Reprinted by permission.

feared and actively hated on every continent. What he stood for—or was thought to stand for—seemed so ominous to Europeans that Winston Churchill felt constrained to work an anti-McCarthy passage into Elizabeth II's Coronation speech, and the *Times* of London observed that "the fears and suspicions which center around the personality of Senator McCarthy are now real enough to count as an essential factor in policy-making for the West."

At home, he was greatly feared and greatly admired. From the president on down, no prudent member of the Truman administration in its last two years, or of the Eisenhower administration in its first two, took any important decision without calculating the likely response of Joe McCarthy. After a bitter wrangle with McCarthy over the Senate's confirmation of Charles E. Bohlen, today our Ambassador to France, as Ambassador to the Soviet Union, Robert A. Taft, the leader of the Republican majority in the Senate, told President Eisenhower that he would not again do battle in behalf of anyone McCarthy opposed.

During the months in which the first Republican administration in twenty years was setting itself up in business, McCarthy held a veto power over appointments.

Many of his colleagues in the Senate convinced themselves that he could determine the outcome of elections. On this the evidence was inconclusive; the chances are that his powers were somewhat overrated.

It was nevertheless a fact that in the elections of 1950 some senators who had been critical of McCarthy lost their seats, and for the next four years there was scarcely any senatorial criticism of him. Few spoke well of him, but fewer still spoke ill of him—until at last the day came when the president of the United States decided that McCarthy threatened the morale of the United States Army and gave the first signal for resistance.

Whatever his impact on elections, he enjoyed, throughout this period, an astonishing and alarming amount of approbation in the country at large. Although his personal following—those who were pleased to think of themselves as "McCarthyites," those who, like William F. Buckley Jr., could hold that "McCarthyism . . . is a movement around which men of good will and stern morality can close ranks"—was never large enough to seem menacing, it was found by the Gallup Poll early in 1954 that 50 percent of Americans held a "favorable opinion" of him, while only 29 percent held an "unfavorable opinion." By early 1954, it should be noted, he had accused the administrations of both Truman and Eisenhower of "treason." And he had said of General of the Army George Catlett Marshall, who up to that moment had seemed the least assailable American of his time, that he was "a man steeped in falsehood . . . who has recourse to the lie whenever it suits his convenience," that he was part of "a conspiracy so infamous, so immense and an infamy so black as to dwarf any previous venture in the history of man," and that he "would sell his grandmother for any advantage." Millions loved it and cried for more.

In "Orestes," Euripides says of the demagogue that he is "a man of loose tongue, intemperate, trusting in tumult, leading the populace to mischief with empty words." McCarthy was all of this. But he differed from the classic model in some striking and important ways. Throughout history, the demagogue's empty words have conveyed empty promises. What demagogues promise and cannot deliver is a future more desirable than the present. The range is from amelioration at one end of the scale to glory at the other. Some offer both and a bit of everything in between. Hitler promised the Germans an improvement in their individual lives and high adventure and conquest as citizens of his Reich. In this country, Huey Long promised to "share the wealth"—when there was little wealth to share—and thereby to make "every man a king."

Demagogy almost always involves the exploitation of desires for at least a somewhat better life and of dreams of downright grandeur. But McCarthy promised no one anything. The only dreams he exploited were bad ones, nightmares. He never sought to rouse his particular rabble by telling them how wretched their present lives were and what hope there was for the future if only they would follow him to his appointed destination. He offered nothing. He had no destination. He was not going anywhere. He had no program of any kind.

He exploited only fears. All demagogues, of course, do this—it is inseparable from their exploitation of hopes. Like most twentieth-century demagogues (except, of course, such as Stalin and Mao Tse-tung and Castro) McCarthy seized on the fear of communism. But he did not do it in the usual way. He never dealt with communism as revolution, as a threat to American society. He did not share the concerns of the House Committee on Un-American Activities over subversion, over the undermining of American institutions. He once halfheartedly undertook an investigation of the press and called it off when the first witness, James Wechsler, of the *New York Post*, proved impossible to browbeat. And he stopped another investigation—this time of communism in education—because the first witness scheduled to testify had to stay home to nurse a bad cold.

Another time, one of his aides kicked up a row with a magazine article which argued that the country's Protestant churches were in grave danger because of the Bolshevik penetration of the clergy. This offended a good many people, including President Eisenhower. McCarthy, who was often extravagantly loyal in support of those who had thrown in their lot with him, made only the feeblest effort to defend this staff member. The Protestant president said he was sure that American clergymen were as incorruptible as ever, and the Catholic senator held his tongue and let the man be cashiered.

McCarthy's interests lay elsewhere. They lay, to be specific, in foreign policy. From the day he stood up in Wheeling until the day he was put down in the Senate, he had nothing to say except that Communists were, as he had charged in Wheeling, "making policy" in those agencies of government that were primarily responsible for our undertakings abroad—the Departments of State and Defense, the United States Information Service, the Central Intelligence Agency. Here, of course, was pay dirt. The cold war was three years old. Four months after Wheeling, our troops were locked in battle with a Communist army in Korea. In New York Federal Court, a former State Department officer had recently been convicted of perjury for having denied involvement in a conspiracy to provide the Soviet Union with state secrets. Before long, there were to be convictions of persons charged with having provided the Russians with scientific intelligence about our atomic installations. This was a very edgy country before McCarthy came along to make it edgier still. If he was going to have but a single string to his demagogic bow, he had chosen the best one.

Nevertheless, it seems to me that the fact of the single string is central to any examination of McCarthy's failures as well as his successes, his weakness as well as his strength in the practice of demagogy. For purposes of examination, I will assume that the end sought by any demagogue—or any politician, for that matter—is power, by which is meant the ability to control people or events or both. In McCarthy's case, I am not sure that this was ever true. If he had personal ambitions of any kind—to be president of the United States, for example—he never did anything to advance them. His friend and lawyer, Edward Bennett Williams, always insisted that he sought not power but glory. I doubt this too. I think that he wanted little more than to be able to stand back and look upon the mischief and tumult and confusion that were his own handiwork, that he was really a rebel without a cause. But he operated within the framework of power, and he used the instruments of power, or at least some of them. His collapse after the Senate censure of 1954 was, I think, a consequence of his failure to exploit hopes and dreams as well as fears and suspicions.

McCarthy was a leader who had a following but not a movement. Not until shortly before the censure vote did he or any of his followers ever attempt to build an organization of any sort, and the one they did set up—a Committee of Ten Million Americans Mobilizing for Justice—had as its only purpose the presentation to the Senate of a petition protesting what was by then the inevitable resolution of censure. (On the day of the vote, it was delivered to the capitol in a Brink's armored truck; it was said to have 1,000,816 signatures.) In point of fact, there was nothing else to base a movement on. It would have been impossible to organize around the single proposition that agents of a foreign power should not be making American policy and that they should, as McCarthy kept saying, be "ferreted out." Ferreting of that sort is a job for government itself, for the president, for the FBI. There is no way for the mass to participate in such a purge.

Had he really wished to build a movement, he might have tied anticommunism to other issues of a more traditional sort. He could, for instance, have argued that the Communist conspiracy to infiltrate the government threatened the livelihood of every non-Communist civil servant. He could have made himself the letter-carrier's friend, the government clerk's protector. There was a good deal of McCarthyism in some parts of the labor movement; he might have sought allies in the trade unions. Since he had no ideological commitments, he could have moved in almost any direction. Though many people today think of him as having been a rightist, an early Bircher, he was in fact nothing of the sort; on domestic issues he voted with the liberals as often as with the conservatives. Had he chosen to do so, he could easily have cooked up some kind of scheme that would have nourished the hopes and the egos of those who accepted his leadership.

If he had done anything of this sort, he would, I feel sure, have survived the Senate's censure and made great capital of it. It is not characteristic of demagogues to collapse when they are rebuffed by the establishment. All that McCarthy had lost, really, was the chairmanship of the Committee on Government Operations. That had been an important source of his power for two of the years in which he had been a great force in American politics. But he had ascended the heights two years before attaining that chairmanship, when he was just one senator in ninety-six and at that a member of the minority party and very low in seniority. Had he ever built a real movement, he could have fired the energies of its members with this new grievance and have threatened his fellow senators as he had done when he had no powers except those of his loose tongue. Instead he went into retirement and talked about moving to Arizona and ending his days with a country law practice and a small ranch.

In his failure to trade on hopes as well as on fears lay his weakness as a demagogue. But the fatal weakness enables us to take the measure of his remarkable gifts. For it must be remembered that he was by no means the first American who had tried to build a large reputation on anticommunism. The Russian Revolution was in its infancy when politicians in this and other countries began to see the possibilities in Red-hunting. Hamilton Fish, a former congressman from New York, had a go at it in the early twenties. The House Committee on Un-American Activities had its greatest days under the leadership of Martin Dies in the late thirties and early forties. McCarthy never had the field to himself. Yet he played it as no one else ever did. With his one-stringed bow, he became a national and an international figure. He gave his name to an "ism" which even today is often as solemnly discussed and analyzed as Marxism-Leninism or Maoism.

Over the years, many students of McCarthy and McCarthyism have taken the view that in and of himself the man was a phenomenon of no particular significance, that he was an inevitable product of the times, that he merely played a role someone or other was bound to play in those years when the cold war was at its lowest on the European front and a shooting war was in progress on the Asian front. In a famous television review of McCarthy's career, the late Edward R. Murrow said "Cassius was right: The fault, dear Brutus, is not in the stars but in ourselves."

Beyond any doubt he was a product of the times. What man is not? But I persist in the belief that he helped to make the times what they were, that without his singular presence they would have been different. He was an innovator. Perhaps his largest contribution to demagogy was what I, writing about him in the *New Yorker* not long after his Wheeling speech, called the technique of the Multiple Untruth. Hitler had instructed the world in the uses of the Big Lie. The Big Lie can be put across in a closed society, but in an open society, with a free press and legislative investigations of the kind that not even McCarthy could completely compromise or corrupt, it is difficult to sustain. McCarthy discovered the value of numbers. Had he said in Wheeling or at any point during his career that there was one Communist or two or even five or six, in this or that agency, his bluff could quite easily have been called but he used large figures and kept changing them. After his Wheeling speech, of which no transcript was ever found, there was some dispute over the number of Communists he had said were on his "list—it turned out not to be a list but a copy of an old letter from a former secretary of state to a congressman—but the highest figure he used was 205, the lowest 57. These were numbers with built-in safety. Showing him to be wrong about three or four of them proved little—what of the other 200 or so, what of the remaining 50-odd?

No one could ever say that he was altogether wrong, or even mostly wrong. Within what appeared to be the Multiple Untruth there might have been—there probably were—some bits and pieces of truth. The Multiple Untruth places an unbearable burden of disproof on the challenger. The work of refutation is always inconclusive, confusing, and—most important of all perhaps—boring to the public. A profusion of names and accusations is exciting. It can be grasped in a single newspaper story. But a hundred newspaper stories, a hundred counteraccusations are simply tiresome, soporific, and unconvincing.

In his promulgation of the Multiple Untruth, McCarthy used, to great and at times quite amusing effect, many of the trappings of scholarship, of research. The bulging briefcase was his symbol. He was rarely seen without one. Inside were photostats, transcripts, clippings, copies of other people's correspondence, and assorted "documents." I met him for the first time a year or so before his rise to fame, and he was trying to persuade me of the soundness of the stand he was taking on a matter that had nothing to do with communism. In his office, he produced for my enlightenment great stacks of papers. No enlightenment ever came. As I examined the papers he handed me, I grew more and more confused. I could not see their relevance; as he talked, I began to lose the thread of his argument. There was, of course, no thread to find, but it took me hours to discover this. I thought at first that I must be at fault and missing his points. It did not occur to me that a man would surround himself with so much paper, with so many photostats, with trays of index cards unless it all meant something. It took me hours to learn that I had been had—that he was passing off as "research" a mere mess of paper that he or someone else had stacked up so that its sheer existence, its bulk, looked impressive. In time, he was to con half the country as, for a time that day, he had conned me.

There was, to my mind, a kind of genius in this. He saw in total irresponsibility and the hocus-pocus of "documentation" possibilities that no one before him had seen, or at any rate put to such effective use. In the long run, the technique may turn out to be his most enduring and his most lamentable contribution to American life. He developed a style of discourse, or pseudodiscourse, that others are using today and with a degree of success approaching his. The American public has in recent years been offered as serious political commentary several books—on President Kennedy, for example, and on President Johnson, and, most notably, on the Warren Commission and Kennedy's assassination—that exemplify as well as any McCarthy speech the uses of the Multiple Untruth and spurious research tricked up to look like the real thing. It may be argued that this is simply yellow journalism between covers and carrying the endorsement of respected publishers. But the old yellow journalism never used footnotes or bibliographies or any other parts of the apparatus of scholarship. The first book of this sort that I know of is *McCarthyism: The Fight for America*, by Senator Joe McCarthy, a preposterous apologia with more than three footnotes per page citing sources which are mostly nonsources.

There was more to his individual style than his technique for misleading by means of the Multiple Untruth. He deliberately created about his own person an atmosphere of violence, of ugliness, of threat. He shrewdly saw that while Americans like to think of themselves as being imbued with a sense of fair play, there exists among us also a sneaking admiration for the "dirty player," the athlete who gets rough in the clinches and scrimmage, who will put the knee to the groin if that is what it takes to win the fight or the game. He never bothered to deny that he had let Robert T. Stevens, Eisenhower's secretary of the Army, know that he would "kick his brains out" if Stevens failed to get in line. He once said to a crowd in Wisconsin, "If you will get me a slippery-elm club and put me aboard Adlai Stevenson's campaign train, I will use it on some of his advisers and perhaps make a good American of him."

"Nice guys finish last," Leo Durocher had said. Many politicians acted on this doctrine long before Durocher's terse formulation of it. But no one ever went so far as McCarthy in letting the public know that he did not consider himself a nice guy, in cultivating the image of himself as the dirty player. Many people are persuaded that this was what finally led to his downfall. For 35 days, or a total of 187 hours, in the late spring of 1954, he played the heavy on network television in what came to be known as the "Army-McCarthy hearings"—a marathon of accusation and counteraccusation on the question, which was more often than not lost sight of, of whether McCarthy and one of his aides, Roy Cohn, had been blackmailing the Army in order to force favors for Pvt. David Schine, a former aide and a friend of Cohn's who, despite all kinds of finagling by members of McCarthy's staff, had been caught up in the draft. He glowered through all his hours on camera. He was abusive, threatening, defiant, disorderly. He denounced the president, the Army, the State Department, and at one time or another every one of the senators who were sitting in judgment upon him.

The generally accepted view ever since has been that this astonishing performance was his undoing. It was estimated the audience before which he played was seldom smaller than twenty million and that just about every American, except for a few hermits and expatriates, caught the act at one time or another. The great majority were repelled by it. But before it can be said that this was what finished him it must be acknowledged that McCarthy wasn't running for office and that few demagogues ever worry much about being liked. Fear can serve them as well as favor. There has never been any evidence to suggest that his behavior at the Army-McCarthy hearings lost him any of his real followers. Most of them sat before their television sets and were thrilled as he shouted and screamed and denounced constituted authority. Had he had any real desire to rally them after his 1954 defeats, had he had any organization or any plan for an organization, he could have continued as a power in American politics. He might have lost his Senate seat in 1958. But that was four years off and, besides, what demagogue needs a Senate seat? Thrown out of Argentina and subsequently a refugee from his place of refuge, Juan Perón has continued, from abroad, to inflame followers in his own and half a dozen other countries.

McCarthy took it lying down. He felt he had lost out in the Army-McCarthy hearings. He tried to fight off censure instead of welcoming it and fighting back. Why? It was partly, as I have said, because he had never organized his followers and had never given them anything which might have led them to organize themselves. But this in itself demands explanation. Why had he failed to offer more? The answer, in my opinion, is that he himself never believed in anything. He was the purest of cynics, and pure cynics are a very rare breed. McCarthy never seemed to believe in himself or in anything he had said. He knew that Communists were not in charge of American foreign policy. He knew that they weren't running the United States Army. He knew that he had spent five years looking for Communists in the government and that—although some must certainly have been there, since Communists had turned up in practically every other major government in the world—he hadn't come up with even one.

His basic weakness, and it is one for which the Republic may be properly grateful, was a lack of seriousness. His only discernible end was mischief. When he had exhausted the possibilities for mischief in any given investigation, he lost interest. He announced that there were Communists "with a razor poised over the jugular vein" in radar laboratories and defense plants. This got big headlines for a while, but when the type grew smaller he moved on to something else, with the razor still poised, the vein still vulnerable. He said that the "worst situation" of all existed in the Central Intelligence Agency, where by his count there were more than "100 Communists."

The Eisenhower administration was at that time giving him a free hand almost everywhere. But as he advanced upon the CIA, the administration grew nervous. To head McCarthy off, the president appointed a commission under General Mark Clark to look into the CIA. The Clark investigation turned up nothing. McCarthy, seeing that the situation might get a bit sticky if he pushed for his own investigation, did nothing. "I guess I'll skip it," he said, letting the "worst situation" prevail and the 100 Communists remain. Knowing what we now know, it is easy to see why the administration was so eager to keep him out of the CIA. Ironically, he might have saved a lot of people a lot of embarrassment if he had bulled his way in and found out what kind of deals the CIA was making with non-governmental organizations. It was just about then, in 1953, that the first of those arrangements were being made.

How much further could he have gone if he had been really serious about it? We Americans have very little experience on which to base any judgment. There were demagogues before McCarthy but they were regional figures for the most part or religious sectarians. In a brilliant essay on demagogy in "The American Democrat," James Fenimore Cooper spoke of the demagogue as if he were by definition a spokesman for some regional interest against the common good—as for example, "the town demagogue" and "the county demagogue." McCarthy was our first national demagogue. He was the first, and thus far the only one, to find a national audience and to seize upon a truly national issue, foreign policy. He surfaced in a period when national and international issues were becoming the dominant ones in American politics and when advances in communications were making it possible for a man to reach a national audience in a relatively short period of time.

He could certainly, I think, have stayed around longer and made more trouble than he did. Five years is a very short time in which to see the beginning and the ending of a gifted politician's career. My general feeling has always been that while he could have stayed on and kept on stirring up confusion, he had already done about all the damage he could do to the system itself. For the system at last turned against him, as it simply had to. Eisenhower had very much wanted to avoid a showdown, but after only a year this proved impossible. McCarthy, a chronic oppositionist, had to turn against his own party and his own administration, and once he did the administration had to fight back. It did not cover itself with glory in its resistance, but it did resist. The Senate, too, feared a confrontation, but the day came when he gave it no choice. Some historians say that American institutions showed up rather badly in meeting the challenge he offered. Some assuredly did. The mass media often truckled to him. The big wheels in Hollywood and on Madison Avenue were scared stiff of him. Manufacturers fearing boycotts from his supporters were careful to give no cause for offense.

For the most part, though, the institutions that allowed themselves to be bullied by him had never been noted for stiffness of spine. Many of them were in the pandering business and survived by seeking to satisfy every taste and give no customer cause for resentment. But other institutions came off quite well. Even while he stormed on Capitol Hill and trampled on the rights of witnesses, the Supreme Court was strengthening individual rights and arming his victims for their own resistance. Most of those newspapers and magazines that were anything more than extensions of the mass entertainment industry exposed and opposed him at every turn. In the academic and intellectual communities, it would have taken more courage to defend him than to attack him. The churches in the main threw their weight against him, and so, with certain exceptions, did the trade unions. None of this, of course, was much consolation to those in the government whose careers he had ruined or those outside the government whose reputations he had sought to blacken. But the best of American institutions held firm, and the threat was at last turned back.

It would be harder to turn back an equally gifted and more determined man in a more desperate time. Since his day no one of comparable talents has appeared. But a more desperate time may one day be upon us and offer similar opportunities for demagogy, and there will be demagogues, perhaps even more gifted, who will try to seize them.

Suggestions for Additional Reading

The roots of the Communist controversies of the 1940s and 1950s are in the 1930s when federal employment expanded and the Communist party temporarily abandoned its public policy of hostility toward liberal democratic institutions. The best historical work on the New Deal and its background is that of Arthur M. Schlesinger, Jr., of which three volumes have been published. See the second of these, *The Coming of the New Deal* (Boston, 1959) passim for references to the Communists of the early 1930s. A journalistic account of the Communist movement in the United States in the 1930s, with special reference to front organizations, is that of Eugene Lyons, *The Red Decade* (Indianapolis, 1941).

Three good histories of the American Communist party are those of Theodore Draper, *The Roots of American Communism* (New York, 1957), for the 1920s; Irving Howe and Lewis Coser, *The American Communist Party* (Boston, 1957) for a general survey; and David A. Shannon, *The Decline of American Communism* (New York, 1959) for the period after the Second World War. For a Communist statement about the American party written in the Popular Front style of the mid-thirties, there is Earl Browder, *What Is Communism?* (New York, 1936). For a Communist statement about the American party written in the cold war style of the late forties and fifties, see William Z. Foster, *History of the Communist Party in the United States* (New York, 1952). Personal accounts of their activity by former members of the Communist party in the thirties and forties are supplied by Benjamin Gitlow, *I Confess* (New York, 1940) and *The Whole of Their Lives* (New York, 1948); and John Gates, *The Story of an American Communist* (New York, 1958).

The presence of Communists in federal employment became a matter of sharp political agitation by congressional committees with the disclosure by Whittaker Chambers and Elizabeth Bentley, in the summer of 1948, that they had been members of separate espionage rings. For their congressional testimony see 80th Congress, 2d Session, House of Representatives, Committee on Un-American Activities, *Hearings Regarding Communist Espionage in the United States Government.* See also Whittaker Chambers, *Witness* (New York, 1952) and Elizabeth Bentley, *Out of Bondage* (New York, 1951). Another account of espionage activity is that of Hede Massing,

This Deception (New York, 1951). Mrs. Massing was the former wife of Gerhardt Eisler, who was to flee the United States and become the propaganda specialist for the East German regime.

There are secondary works on Communist activity in the United States, most of which are based upon the records of congressional committees. Among these is James Burnham, *The Web of Subversion* (New York, 1954). An estimation of Soviet espionage throughout the world, with a chapter on the United States, is David J. Dallin, *Soviet Espionage* (New Haven, 1955). Earlier works on atomic espionage in the United States are Alan Morehead, *The Traitors* (New York, 1952) and Oliver Pilat, *The Atom Spies* (New York, 1952). The Morehead book was republished in 1963 with a new preface. Also published in 1963 was Ralph de Toledano, *The Greatest Plot in History* (New York, 1963). For an exposition of the view that there was no atomic secret and no atom spy plot, and that the whole affair was the manufacture of militarists, politicians, and financiers fighting against peace, see William A. Reuben, *The Atom Spy Hoax* (New York, 1955). For statements of opinion that the Rosenbergs were unjustly convicted and executed, see John Wexley, *The Judgment of Julius and Ethel Rosenberg* (New York, 1955) and Walter and Miriam Schneir, *Invitation to an Inquest* (Garden City, N.Y., 1965).

An extensive statement about the controversy over communism from the New Deal to the condemnation of McCarthy is Earl Latham, *The Communist Controversy in Washington: From the New Deal to McCarthy* (Cambridge, 1966). An account of President Truman's handling of certain aspects of the Communist issue is that of Alan D. Harper, *The Politics of Loyalty: The White House and the Communist Issue, 1946–1952* (Westport, Conn., 1969).

A somewhat subjective statement of events in 1954 of which Senator McCarthy was the center is Senator Charles E. Potter, *Days of Shame* (New York, 1965). A useful examination of the McCarthy phenomenon is Michael Paul Rogin, *The Intellectuals and McCarthy: The Radical Specter* (Cambridge, 1967). For revisionist interpretations of McCarthyism, see Athan Theoharis, *Seeds of Repression, Harry S. Truman and the Origins of McCarthyism* (Chicago: 1971) and Richard M. Freeland, *The Truman Doctrine and the Origins of McCarthyism* (New York, 1971), the gravamen of which seems to be that President Truman was responsible for McCarthyism. Many of those accused before congressional committees, or who were thought to have suffered duress in loyalty and security proceedings, wrote books about their experiences or became the subjects of books. On the case of Alger Hiss, see the following: Alistair Cook, *Generation on Trial* (New York, 1950); Lord Jowitt, *The Strange Case of Alger Hiss* (New York, 1953); Alger Hiss, *In the Court of Public Opinion* (New York, 1957); Fred J. Cook, *The Unfinished Story of Alger Hiss* (New York, 1958). Richard M. Nixon also discussed the Hiss investigation of which he was a part in *Six Crises* (New York, 1962). As to other figures in congressional or loyalty proceedings, there are: Charles P. Curtis, *The Oppenheimer Case* (New York, 1955); Nathan I. White, *Harry Dexter White, Loyal American* (Waban, Massachusetts, 1956); Philip Wittenberg (ed.), *The Lamont Case* (New York, 1957); Owen D. Lattimore, *Ordeal by Slander* (Boston, 1950). For biographical sketches of some who were in or close to the Communist movement at some time, see Murray Kempton, *Part of Our Time* (New York, 1955).

The congressional committees were strongly attacked by some critics. Among these were Alan Barth, *Government by Investigation* (New York, 1955); Telford Taylor, *Grand Inquest* (New York, 1955); Robert K. Carr, *The House Committee on Un-American Activities* (Ithaca, 1952); and Frank J. Donner, *The Un-Americans* (New York, 1961). A strong defense of the committees is that of William F. Buckley, Jr., *The Committee and Its Critics* (New York, 1962). A balanced account is that of Walter Goodman, *The Committee: The Extraordinary Career of the House Committee on Un-American Activities* (New York, 1967). The problem of the credibility of some witnesses in congressional proceedings is raised by the confession of Harvey Matusow, *False Witness* (New York, 1955); and is analyzed in Herbert L. Packer, *Ex-Communist Witnesses* (Stanford, 1962). The delicate and difficult questions involved in balancing individual rights and national security are weighed in Morton Grodzins, *The Loyal and the Disloyal* (Chicago, 1956); Edward A. Shils, *The Torment of Secrecy* (Glencoe, Illinois, 1956); and especially, Ralph S. Brown, Jr., *Loyalty and Security* (New Haven, 1958).

The most assiduous expositor of Senator McCarthy's views was the senator himself, both in print and in hearings. In print, see Senator Joe McCarthy, *McCarthyism, the Fight for America* (New York, 1952). The most notable of the hearings over which he presided were those involving the Voice of America and the overseas information centers of the State Department. See 83rd Congress, 1st Session, United States Senate, Committee on Government Operations, Permanent Subcommittee on Investigations, *Hearings Pursuant to S. Res. 40, State Department Information Program—Voice of America.* Two people who were aggrieved by Senator McCarthy in the course of these hearings and told of their experiences were Martin Merson, *The Private Diary of a Public Servant* (New York, 1955) and James A. Wechsler, *The Age of Suspicion* (New York, 1953). Hearings in which Senator McCarthy was the chief antagonist were those headed by Senator Millard Tydings of Maryland to assess the Wisconsin Senator's charges against the State Department, 81st Congress, 2d Session, United States Senate, Subcommittee of the Committee on Foreign Relations, *Hearings Pursuant to S. Res. 231.* The best-known hearings in which Senator McCarthy played a part were undoubtedly those called to ascertain the truth of mutual charges and recriminations between the senator and the Pentagon, 83rd Congress, 2d Session, United States Senate, Committee on Government Operations, Special Subcommittee on Investigations, *Special Senate Investigation of Charges and Counter-charges Involving: Secretary of the Army Robert T. Stevens, John G. Adams, H. Struve Hensel and Senator Joe McCarthy, Roy M. Cohn, and Francis P. Carr, Hearings.*

Certain special perspectives may also be of interest. For example, a writer in a leading Catholic publication took a strongly critical position for which see John Cogley, "McCarthyism Revisited," *The Commonweal* 62, no. 7, May 20, 1955 and "Behind the Many Faces," *The Commonweal* 62, no. 6, May 13, 1955. A historian saw Senator McCarthy as a man essentially of the Left representing a special kind of Jacobinism, Peter Viereck, "The New American Radicals," *The Reporter* 11, 12, December 30, 1954. Although the arousal over communism was of enormous concern to governmental and professional people, the evidence is that the great body of the people were largely undisturbed. See the findings of an extensive survey to measure the impact of McCarthyism in the country as reported in Samuel A. Stouffer, *Communism, Conformity, and Civil Liberties* (New York, 1955).

18-302